W9-DHK-514

973.27   134523
Cre
Jac

Jacob.
A biographical sketch of the life
of the late Captain Michael
Cresap.

Learning Resources Center

Nazareth College of Rochester, N. Y.

The First

American Frontier

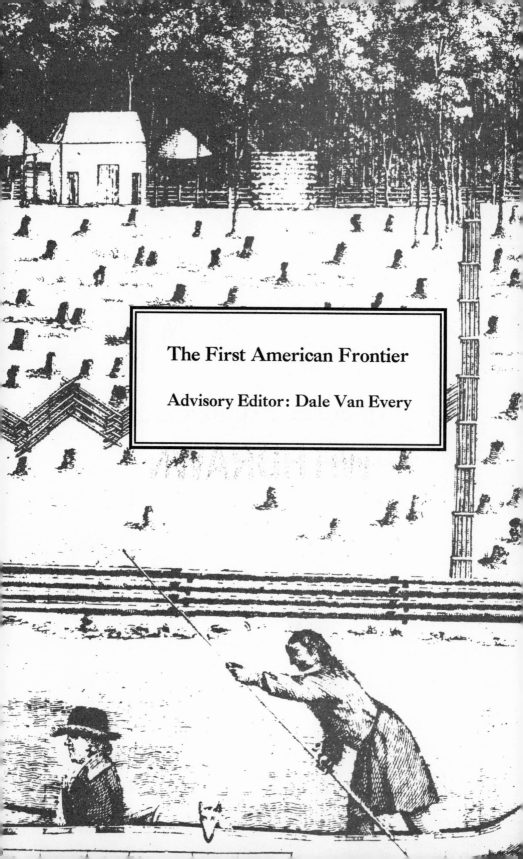

The First American Frontier

Advisory Editor: Dale Van Every

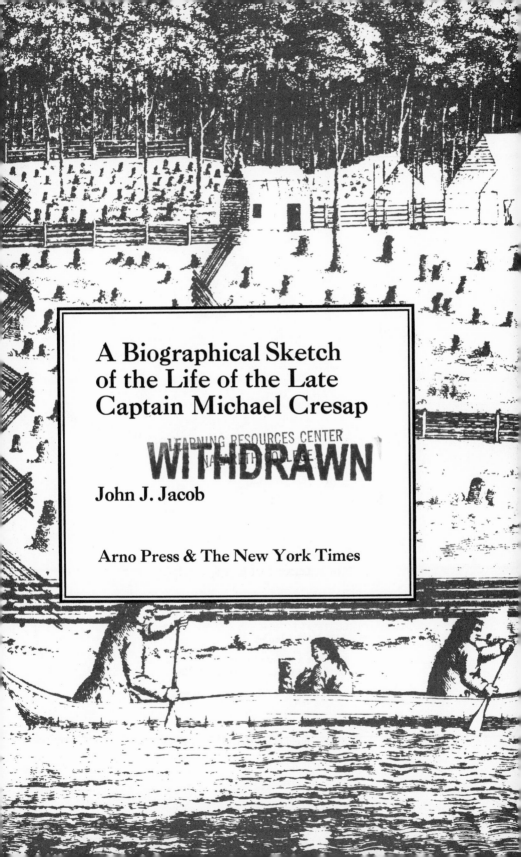

A Biographical Sketch
of the Life of the Late
Captain Michael Cresap

LEARNING RESOURCES CENTER

WITHDRAWN

John J. Jacob

Arno Press & The New York Times

134523

Reprint Edition 1971 by Arno Press Inc.

Reprinted from a copy in
The State Historical Society of Wisconsin Library

LC #   73-146404
ISBN 0-405-02863-6

The First American Frontier
ISBN for complete set: 0-405-02820-2

See last pages of this volume for titles.

Manufactured in the United States of America

973.27
Cre
Jac

A

BIOGRAPHICAL SKETCH

OF THE

Life of the Late

CAPTAIN MICHAEL CRESAP.

I appeal to the White Man ungrateful, to say,
If he e'er from my Cabin went hungry away?
If naked and cold unto Logan he came,
And he gave him no blanket, and kindled no flame?"

By *JOHN J. JACOB.*

Cincinnati, Ohio:

Re-printed from the *Cumberland Edition* of 1826, with *Notes* and *Appendix* for
WILLIAM DODGE, by JNO. F. UHLHORN, Steam Job Printer, 58 West 3d St.

1866.

ADVERTISEMENT.

I think it necessary, as the name of Mr. Jefferson is introduced into this work, to inform the reader that it was finished and sent to the press as early as March last; but from circumstances not within the control of the author, has remained to this late period silently on the printer's shelves. The author gives this notice, lest it should be thought ungenerous, if not invidious, to call in question any statement of facts made by a man now dead, and incapable of making any reply.

September 25, 1826.

HON. JOHN E. HOWARD, Esq.,

Late Governor of Maryland,

And the rest of my compatriots and grey-headed fellow-sufferers—
the surviving Officers of the Revolutionary War:

Gentlemen: From the nature of the subject of the following memoir, as well as from that cordial and sincere affection I feel as a fellow-soldier, I take the liberty of dedicating to you the following sheets, containing a short narrative and defense of the character of not only a soldier but a hero.

Accept, gentlemen, this first and last and only pledge in my power of an unceasing friendship—begotten in youth, strengthened by mutual sufferings, and matured with old age.

It is doubtless an unpleasant reflection, that now in the decline of life we are placed in such circumstances as to preclude all the endearments connected with social intercourse. We can, however, collect our neighboring youth around us, and fight our battles o'er and o'er again, by our firesides; and when left alone, like Uncle Toby, build forts with brickbats and lay sieges with wooden guns and hickory sticks.

And, gentlemen, although I feel no disposition to involve or identify you in a controversy of this kind—a controversy in which you, perhaps, feel but little interest—yet permit me to observe that, in a national view, it is a controversy in which we are all in some degree involved; because it is not the family of Captain Cresap only, but all the officers of the army, the State of Maryland, and the National character that are at stake; for it will not be forgotten that Captain Cresap was the first captain selected by the State of Maryland in the Revolutionary war.

It is, then, I conceive, a poor compliment to the officers of the army, and especially to Maryland, to say, or permit it to be said, that an *"infamous murderer"* was selected as one of her distinguished citizens by the State of Maryland, to fill the most honorable military station in her gift.

If, then, gentlemen, I am so happy as to be able to remove this stigma, and expunge all those black spots imputed to Captain Cresap, I certainly render my country a service.

And I sincerely pray, gentlemen, that you and each of you may now, in the decline of life, enjoy all that felicity, ease, prosperity and happiness that your services merit and your age and infirmities require; and may none of us in a dying hour have it to say, from penury and want, what was pathetically the dying dirge of poor old Wolsey: "If," said he, "I had served my God as faithfully as my King (country), he would not have forsaken me in my last moments."

THE AUTHOR.

PREFACE.

Soon after Mr. Jefferson's celebrated Notes were published, or rather soon after I became acquainted with them, I conceived the design of refuting the unfounded and unjust charges therein against my deceased friend Captain Michael Cresap*—knowing most assuredly from personal acquaintance with the accused that those charges were not true. But I foresaw, from the celebrity of the author of the Notes on Virginia—not only as a man of superior talents, but as standing high, yea, pre-eminent in the estimation of his fellow-citizens as a politician—I foresaw, I say, to call in question the truth of any statement made by such a man, especially by such a pigmy as myself, however encircled with the shield of truth, would in all probability be as unavailing and feeble as the efforts of a mosquito to demolish an ox.

Thus perplexed, and doubtful what course to pursue, I received an assurance from Luther Martin, Esq., Attorney General of Maryland, who had intermarried with a daughter of Captain Cresap, that he would undertake a defense of his character. This assurance of Mr. Martin relieved my mind, feeling confident as to the result, knowing him not only to possess superior talents, but occupying a station and moving in a circle co-equal in respectability with the Philosopher of Monticello. I therefore, without delay, placed in his hands the materials for the work (as they were in my possession). Mr.

---

*Mr. Jefferson calls him Colonel Michael Cresap—which mistake, trifling as it may appear, yet goes to prove the imperfect acquaintance he had with the man and the character he handles so freely. It is true there was a colonel of this name, but everybody knows he was not the man intended.

Martin soon after published, in pamphlet form, the defense of Captain Cresap's character, but it had not the desired effect; first, because it was not, nor could in its nature be coextensive with the Notes on Virginia; secondly, pamphlets, after the first reading, are thrown aside, lost and forgotten. And permit me to add, thirdly, that at the period when Mr. Martin's piece issued from the press politics ran high, party spirit was hot, and Mr. Jefferson's name stood highest among his brethren of the great and respectable Republican party. It was but too evident that any blemish on the moral fame of such a man was easily transferable to his political standing; hence it was better upon the whole, some men might think, that Cresap, however innocent, should yet remain under censure than that any suspicion as to the perfection of so great a character should rest on the public mind. Since which period, regardless of truth, honor and justice, a great many orators, poets and scribblers have been dashing away at the name, and fame, and character of a man of whom it is presumable they know just about as much as of Kouli Khan or prester John, and who was as much their superior as the noble lion is to the muskrat. All these little folks, I knew, would soon sink into the dusky shades of oblivion, and therefore regarded them as squibs of smoke that the wind would carry away.

But a book has lately fallen into my hands, written by Rev. Dr. Doddridge of Wellsburg, a man for whom I had hitherto entertained the highest respect—yea, warmest friendship—in which book, for what cause to me utterly problematical, the old sore is irritated and laid open again. Not only the old Logan speech is raised from the dead, but a new and hitherto unheard-of charge leveled against the character and fame of Captain Cresap. It therefore now becomes my indispensable and imperative duty, however late, as the only remaining person on earth qualified from personal knowledge to do that justice to the memory of this mistaken and abused character that I think no other individual can do, and which, in fact, has been too long delayed.

The piece published some years since by Mr. Martin aimed at nothing more than a refutation of the charges brought against Captain Cresap in the celebrated Notes on Virginia, to-wit: the Logan speech, and Mr. Jefferson's superaddition, that he (Captain Cresap) "*was infamous for his many Indian murders.*" Now, however conclusive and satisfactory the facts and arguments, as stated in Mr. Martin's piece, might appear to men of candor at the time that piece appeared in public, yet it is believed that at this day scarcely a vestige remains, nor do I know where I should apply successfully for a copy. Hence my plan is different. I mean, in order the more effectually to put to silence forever all his calumniators and adversaries, to bring into public view all the life of the late Captain Michael Cresap deemed necessary not only to refute the charges against him, but to evince and demonstrate to the world that they have been imposed upon, and greatly deceived in the man. But my task is difficult: to prove a negative is no easy matter; nor can it be done in any other way than by producing positive proof that positive charges cannot be true; and in this case the various circumstances combined with the weight of testimony must decide.

The name and fame of Hector and Achilles live only in the poems of Homer; nor would a Phocion or Caius Gracchus have been heard of in succeeding ages without a Plutarch. What a pity a greater man than either should have so poor a biographer!

JOHN J. JACOB.

March 10, 1826.

INTRODUCTION.

It may, perhaps, be satisfactory to the readers to hear something of the competency and qualification of the author for a work of this kind; indeed, in my view it is all important. I therefore beg leave to state that I became an inmate of the family of Captain Cresap in my fifteenth year, and soon after, although very young, had the principal charge of his store; and such was his confidence in me, that about one year after he branched out his goods and sent me to a stand he had selected in the Allegheny Mountains, with a small assortment. The next year, to-wit: 1774, he sent me still further west, to-wit: to the place now called Brownsville, with a pretty large cargo. This whole cargo, in consequence of his instructions, I sold to the officers and soldiers in the Virginia service, in Dunmore's war. This store being dissolved, I returned to his family, at his residence in Oldtown, now Allegheny county, Maryland. Early in the year 1775 Captain Cresap marched to Boston with a company of riflemen, and committed all his intricate and multifarious business to my care. I was then eighteen years old. Dunmore's war being over, the colony of Virginia (for such she then was) appointed Commissioners to settle the expenses thereof, to-wit: Richard Lee, Esq., Colonel Henry Lee, Colonel Clapham, Colonel Blackburn and Colonel F. Payton. These gentlemen sat at Pittsburg, Redstone, Old Fort and Winchester, at all of which places I attended. The gentlemen composing this board were remarkably kind and accommodating to me; they called me young Cresap, and allowed me a table and chair near them—the consequence of which was, that when any of the captains or officers appeared on whom I had claims for Captain Cresap, the Commissioners first deducted my claims out of their pay, and gave me a certificate for the amount; and if, as it sometimes happened, a dispute arose between these officers and myself, the Commissioners would laugh, and I believe invariably decided in my favor. Thus, through my persevering diligence and the accommodating spirit of the Commissioners, I obtained for Captain Cresap during his absence drafts on the Treasury of Virginia to a large amount, and was delighted with the prospect of presenting him with such a handsome sum of money on his return home; but, unhappily for his family, he never did return. My hopes perished, and I felt as an orphan cast upon an unfriendly world without father, mother or friend. I remained, however, with the widow and family until about the first of July, 1776, when, being now nineteen years old, I was selected as the ensign to a company of militia, ordered to march to General Washington's camp. These militia, when collected together, amounted to about 1,500 men, from the State of Maryland, commanded by General Beale, and were called the Flying Camp. We arrived at Fort Lee, on the west side of the Hudson river, just in time to see Fort Washington, on the opposite shore, taken by the British. The next day, I believe, or very soon after, we retraced our steps, and had a tag-rag race through the Jerseys, with General Howe and the English army at our heels; and we proved that, however much the British might be over our match in some things, yet there was one thing in which we beat them — namely, in running! We reached Philadelphia in safety early in December, and were discharged; but I applied for a commission in the regular army and was appointed a lieutenant, and remained in the army during five campaigns, to-wit: until the Winter of 1781. I then retired, as the Maryland line had suffered greatly, and was much reduced in the fatal battle of Camden, in South Carolina. And I think it was in the Summer or Autumn of this year, 1781, that I was married to Captain Cresap's widow, with whom I lived near forty years. Thus it will appear, from my intimate acquaintance with Captain Cresap from the year 1772 to his death—from my intermarriage with his widow, with whom I lived a great many years—from the circumstance of all his papers, books and memorandums falling into my hands, and, permit me to add, from that implicit and unbounded confidence he placed in me—it must be evident to every man that no part of his public life was or could have been concealed from me. Captain Cresap was naturally cheerful, full of vivacity, and very communicative; and I am certain that there was no occurrence, no interesting circumstance, especially in respect to the Indians, but what was detailed to his wife, and often in my presence. Therefore, I venture to predict that if any man shall presume to contradict what I shall advance in the following memoirs of the life of Captain Cresap, he must prove that truth is not truth, or that facts are lies.

And with the readers' permission, I will add, that this short narrative of my proceedings, as the clerk or agent of Captain Cresap, with the Virginia Commissioners, furnishes strong presumptive proof that at this period, to-wit: in the Summer and Autumn of the year 1775, no such idea was entertained of Captain Cresap, by the gentlemen who settled the expenses of Dunmore's war, as that he was the murderer of Logan's family, or that he was a man of infamous character as an Indian murderer, or that he was the cause of the war. I say, if those gentlemen had entertained any such idea I should certainly have heard it from some of them, either at Pittsburg, Redstone or Winchester; but I most solemnly declare that I never did, to my knowledge or recollection, hear the least whisper or the smallest intimation of the kind from them, or any other individual; so far from it, that Captain Cresap was treated with the most marked and respectful attention, manifested to me who acted as his representative, although only a boy.

A

BIOGRAPHICAL SKETCH

OF THE LIFE

OF THE LATE

CAPT. MICHAEL CRESAP.

CUMBERLAND, MD.
Printed for the Author, by J. M. Buchanan.

1826.

CHAPTER I.

A concise View of the Customs, Manners and Physical Strength of the American Nation at the commencement of the Revolutionary War.

As nearly every circumstance connected with our late Revolutionary War has already become history, it would be superfluous to attempt a detail of facts already recorded. I mean, therefore, only to make a few remarks, merely with a view to show the perilous state of the Nation when the hero whose life I am endeavoring to portray in its real colors was in his zenith, and actively and almost unremittingly engaged in his country's service.

It is, I believe, historically a fact, that as early as the year 1763 the British Government began to frown and threaten, to stretch out her arbitrary arms and shake them first at her American children. Nor did they stop with words and vaporing, but proceeded to pass what was called the Stamp Act, designed, it is presumed, not only to feel how our pulses beat, but also as an entering wedge to ulterior measures. This law was, however, so unpopular, and met with such resolute and determined opposition that John Bull thought it best at that time to draw in his horns, and the Stamp Act was repealed in March, 1766. It was not, however, as the sequel has proved, an abandonment, but a mere suspension of that correction they were preparing for such a refractory and disobedient set of children; and consequently, in the years 1773 and 1774, they came to the determination to give us such a sound drubbing as to make us mend our manners, or whip us until we did. They now threw away the feelings of a parent and commenced tyrant, and passed several laws subversive of our liberties, and past endurance; and to cap the climax, declared explicitly that they had the right to bind us in all cases whatever. These proceedings and this language were indigestible food to our Yankee stomachs; we would not swallow it, and the Revolutionary War ensued.

I suppose it is with Nations as with individuals, that is to say, while young men continue in their minority they think it no degradation strictly to conform to the laws and rules of parental authority; but when they arrive at maturity of physical and mental powers they become restive, impatient and anxious for freedom and emancipation from the dominion and control of others. And so it is, and so I presume it should be, with Nations who have understanding and energy sufficient to assert and maintain their rights. Some Nations have been handcuffed and fettered until their wrists and ancles have become callous, and they no longer feel their chains; others are so effeminate that, so long as they can eat, and drink, and sleep, they care not who suffers, who governs, and how the world goes; others, again, are so ignorant that they neither know nor care for their rights. But, to the honor of the American name, we have set an example to the world sublime in its nature and imperishable in its effects. The intensity of that sacred flame of patriotism that burnt in the breasts of our old Congresses, revolutionary armies, and Nation at large, has not been nor will be extinguished so long as materials remain in our little world to feed the flame. The southern hemisphere of this vast continent, so long enveloped in a dark cloud of ignorance and superstition, has at length emerged from her long night of abject degradation, and now begins to shine a star in the phalanx of rational liberty. Living coals and sparks of fire occasionally shed a ray of light in the thick fog of enslaved Europe. But the sun will rise in due time, and the fog will be dispersed. Enough of this.

There was one peculiar circumstance in our Revolutionary War, that I believe has not been noticed by any historian: I mean that remarkable Providence that restrained and sus-pended the uplifted arm of vengeance from falling upon us until we were prepared to meet the stroke and repel its force; and if we advert to the state of our population, numerical strength, and to our habits, customs and manners at that period, it would seem that there never could have happened a time more propitious, either in respect to the state of our own country or in reference to the European Governments. Our numerical strength—perhaps about 500,000 fighting men, or men able to bear arms—was now equal to the power of our enemies, fettered and cramped as they were at such a distance from the scene of action, or theater of war. We were, more-over, from habits and manners, prepared and fitted for the tented field. Our young men were vigorous, athletic and act-ive; inured to fatigue, privations and plain living from their infancy, they were prepared to suffer more and complain less than the dandies of the nineteenth century, if placed in similar circumstances. Those days of bacon and cabbage, of hominy and pone, milk and mush, of hunting-shirts, leggings and moc-casins, have passed away; we are now, please your honors, a refined, polished, polite people.

But still, may we not ask the all-important question: First, if the British Nation had struck us somewhat sooner, should we have had strength to repel the blow? And if some thirty or forty years later, are we sure that the Nation at such a period, under the influence of the British Government, and so much older in vice and effeminacy, would have possessed public virtue, patriotism and energy sufficient not only harmoniously and cordially to unite, but energy sufficient to make effectual resistance?

These questions, I know, contain problems not now to be solved; but they point us to a kind Providence for our deliverance. Our Revolutionary War was the womb that gave birth to the Nation. And although many historians have recorded the most prominent and important scenes and circumstances connected therewith, yet I do not remember having seen any history written by a soldier—none written by a man who saw and tasted and felt all the fatigues, privations and sufferings of several campaigns, or even of one campaign, during this period that tried men's souls.*

To enter minutely into a detail of the sufferings of an American soldier of the Revolution would, perhaps, in some cases, appear almost fabulous to the sweet-scented bucks of 1826. We will therefore touch the subject slightly. It is a fact well known, that the prisoners taken at Fort Washington and York Island, in 1776, were crowded in jails and prison-ships, where all suffered severely and many died; that after General Washington commenced his retreat through the States of New York and the Jerseys, at the close of this campaign, to-wit: about the last of November, many of the soldiers were barefoot and nearly naked, and it was said that the army might be traced by their blood.

The campaign of 1777 was emphatically the campaign of suffering, fighting and blood. In it was fought the battles of Brandywine, Germantown and Saratoga, exclusive of smaller affairs. Two of these battles I was personally engaged in, to-wit: Brandywine and Germantown. As to the first, we laid

* I believe Colonel Lee has given us some account of the Southern army.

on our arms all night, and slept little, if any. We fought, or were in our ranks and stations, all day, and the battle ended at night. We then marched in a disorderly manner nearly all night—slept but little, if any, and ate nothing from the night of the 10th of September until some time in the day of the 12th. The army then marched to a place called Red-clay, where we attempted again to give the British army battle, but such a severe storm of cold rain came upon us that each army parted by mutual consent; and so severe was the storm, which continued with unabated fury all night, and the night was so dark, that our baggage wagons could not come up to us; and we laid in this storm without tent, or covering, or food, or fire. I saw, I believe, but one in camp.

On the 3d of October following, we left our camp early in the night and marched to attack the British in Germantown. We arrived and commenced firing at dawn of day. The battle continued with alternate success until 9 or 10 o'clock A. M. We then left the field, at first in tolerable good order; but loss of sleep and want of food had so completely unhinged all our bodily and mental powers, that in spite of all the efforts of the officers the men were continually falling behind, turning into the woods and getting to sleep. Here again we had no opportunity of getting food until in the night of the 4th— about twenty-four hours. At the close of this campaign General Washington built huts or cabins, and went into Winter quarters at a place called Valley Forge, but sent the Maryland line, to which I was attached, to take up their Winter quarters in Wilmington, on the Delaware river. At this period the Maryland line, and I suppose the army in general, were nearly naked; and the main army, who took up their quarters at Valley Forge, were, I believe, without a supply of food for several days. Fortunately, however, the Maryland line fared better, for it so happened that a kind Providence sent us a supply from our enemies. And so remarkable was this circumstance, that it deserves a page in history.

The Maryland line had but just taken possession of the post assigned them for their Winter quarters, which lay upon a hill in view of the river Delaware, on which river the British ships were continually passing up and down, and it so happened that a pretty large brig loaded with the baggage of the British army got aground near the Pennsylvania shore. This was soon discovered, and a party of men with a six-pound field-piece or two were sent to take her. This was easily effected, for she could make no resistance. We found in this brig a great quantity of clothing for officers and soldiers, rum, wine, tea, coffee, sugar, etc., all of which articles were exactly what we needed. This rendered our situation truly comfortable; and the Winter of 1777–'78 was the most pleasant we spent during the whole war.

The campaign of 1778 was more agreeable. We were better fed and clothed, and had only one battle—that of Monmouth, in the month of June, and at this time had the pleasure of beating and driving Sir Harry Clinton and his red-coats off the field. Of the campaign of 1779 I have little to say, because very little was done; but one remark may go to show what must have been the poverty and sufferings of the officers especially. Sometime toward the conclusion of this campaign I took a journey from the Jerseys to Baltimore, at the request of the officers of the regiment, to purchase for them as much cloth as would make each of them a regimental coat of fine blue; this I effected, after a pretty long search in Baltimore before I could find any, and for which I paid the merchant £1,500 for fifteen yards. And this fifteen yards was designed to make ten coats, and ten coats it did make.

The campaign of 1780 fell with peculiar severity on the Maryland line and Delaware regiment always attached to and almost identified with the Maryland troops. Early in the Spring of this year these troops were detached from the grand army and ordered to the Southern Department, under the command of General Baron DeKalb. They marched leisurely and in high glee through Maryland and Virginia, and reached the Carolinas, I believe, toward the last of July. The intense heat of the weather at this season to a Northern people in a Southern climate was extremely unpleasant; yet we had very little sickness and no complaining. We had advanced far into the Southern Carolina when General Gates arrived—perhaps about the 8th or 10th day of August—and took the command in chief. He had no sooner assumed command than he moved the army with great rapidity, presuming, I suppose, that he would surprise Burgoyne, the Earl of Cornwallis. I believe it was in the evening of the 13th or 14th of August we arrived at Rugely's mill, encamped, and were joined, perhaps the next day, by the Virginia militia, said to be 2,000. Our own numbers of regular effective men did not, I think, exceed 1,000. Early in the night of the 15th of August we struck our tents, and marched directly for Camden, to catch Cornwallis napping. But, whether he had any intimation of Gates's design, or whether he had the same design upon him, I know not; but certain it is we met about half way between the two camps at near midnight. The moon shone brightly, and the surprise was mutual. We exchanged a few shots, formed in line of battle, and sat down in our places until day appeared, which no sooner began to dawn than our morning guns on each side, being well charged, were directed at our enemies, which were immediately followed by an incessant roar from the center to each wing of cannon and musketry. It was an open, fine woods, with little undergrowth, and we had no cavalry; and this single circumstance gave the enemy much the advantage. The militia soon fled, but our regular troops, under every possible disadvantage—flanked on the left, which was now deserted by the militia, the Commander-in-Chief gone—maintained their ground until 8 or 9 o'clock A. M.

The Maryland line at this time were generally old veteran soldiers. They could and did defend themselves until so cut up, flanked and surrounded that it was impossible to sustain the shock any longer without the loss of the whole army. Indeed, few were left—not more, I think, than 250 men; and, although we lost the day and most of our army, no blame or censure can, without the greatest injustice, attach to the name of any individual officer or soldier of the Maryland line. Never were a braver set of men—no, never was a better fought battle; and I am under the impression that a better disposition of the army and better generalship, with a few hundred horsemen, would have given us a very different result, the superiority of Cornwallis's army, and the desertion of the militia to the contrary notwithstanding. I saw, in particular, such coolness and personal bravery in General Gist, Colonel Howard and some others—yea, many others—that I am confident upon equal ground we could have fought, and I think subdued an equal number of the best of the British troops. But oh, woful day for Maryland and Delaware! How many weeping wives and mothers who can tell ? We must have lost, in killed, wounded and prisoners, out of our small army, between seven and eight hundred men, General Baron DeKalb and many valuable officers being among the slain.

As every splendid act of heroism deserves a reward, I

think it proper to mention one that deserves notice. After the battle was over, of what troops were left General Small-wood—who commanded the rear line, and who had the brunt and most dreadful part of the battle—collected, with the aid of General Gist and others, about 150 men, and moved west-ward. Colonel Howard, who was among the last that left the field, collected also at first about 50 or 60 men, but which in-creased, I believe, to 80 or 90. With this little company he marched toward the south about five or six miles and then turned westward. I was in this party. About 1 o'clock we halted in the woods to rest—not to eat, for we had nothing of this kind. While lying at this place a soldier who had escaped from the field of battle joined us, and said Captain Somerville, of the Sixth Regiment, was badly wounded and left upon the field. On hearing this Captain Truman said, if Colonel Howard would remain where he then was, and any one individual would go with him, he would go down to the battle field and bring off Somerville. To this proposal Colonel Howard acceded; and one of our party volunteering to go with him, he took a horse, went to the field of battle, found Somerville, and brought him to us in a short time, badly wounded in one arm, which he finally lost by amputation. Many more such interesting anecdotes might be mentioned, but my limits, and the object I have primarily in view, forbid it.

After this battle no poor fellows were in a more destitute and suffering condition. The baggage wagons that were with the army were all taken, all our clothes were lost, very few of the officers having a second shirt. Neither had we food of any kind; we lived on watermelons, peaches, etc., from the night of the 15th of August to the night of the 17th or 18th, I do not recollect which; and then the party I was with

supped upon a cow they killed, without bread, and a very
little salt. As well as I remember—for I was sick and could
eat no supper—they proceeded in the following manner:
They skinned the cow far enough to empty out the intestines,
and then cut off ribs and pieces until they reached the skin,
and then proceeded to skin farther as they wanted. Nor was
our situation much bettered until we reached Hillsborough, in
North Carolina, a distance, I believe, to follow the route we
pursued, of more than two hundred miles. Here we halted,
collected our scattered forces and made a stand. From
this place I was sent to Maryland, as a supernumerary
officer. And here I close my few remarks as to the sufferings
of the army in the war of our Revolution. The narrative is
simply a mere recital of a few facts and incidents, without
any effort to embellish or portray in dark and dismal colors
the sufferings of a meritorious set of men, most of whom
have now sunk into their graves.

Having made these few remarks upon the subject of our
Revolutionary War, we will, with the reader's permission,
bring into view some other circumstances illustrative of the
ground we have taken—namely, that it was a peculiar and
kind Providence that brought upon us the war of the Revolution precisely at the period when we were in circumstances
better, perhaps, than any other to meet and breast the storm.

Among other things of this nature, it was not a small one
that the yeomanry, or men in the middle and lower walks of
life, especially on or near our frontiers, were the best marksmen in the world. An anecdote or two will demonstrate this
fact: I remember when the company commanded by Captain
Cresap lay at Redstone Old Fort, in the time of Dunmore's
war, a buzzard came sailing over us at some considerable
hight, when three men—Daniel Cresap, Joseph Cresap and

William Ogle—all raising their rifles, fired at the same instant. The buzzard fell, and they all declared they had killed it; we examined the buzzard, and found all three of their balls had pierced it. But a more important fact, and one which will not soon be forgotten, was the dreadful havoc made among the Hessians by Colonel Rawlings's Rifle Regiment, at the time Fort Washington and York Island were taken by the British. Captain Cresap also had in his company two brothers of the name of Shain, such unerring marksmen with their rifles that they seldom missed a mark the size of a cent at the distance of twenty or twenty-five yards, off-hand shooting. As I was among these people I heard many tales of this close shooting, but I waive them and proceed.

Let it be remembered that this hardy race of young men and this state of things were not only the result of our peculiar habits and simplicity of manners, but naturally grew out of our wars with the Indians. Our frontier* inhabitants were always exposed to a predatory war with the Indians— not embodied as an army publicly invading our country, but a straggling banditti, attacking individuals and families remote from a dense population. These attacks were often in the night, or just at break of day—sometimes killing all the family, at other times only a part, to-wit: the men and small children, leading the women and elder children captives, but I believe always burning the houses and stealing all the horses. They were, however, sometimes deceived and disappointed—a remarkable instance of which occurred in Kentucky about the time of its first settlement. Five Indians about daybreak attacked the house of a man (if I recollect

---

* What was called "the frontier" was continually changing and diverging westward, so that the habits and feelings of the people remained the same many miles eastward after the frontier was changed.

3

right of the name of Chenoweth). Mr. Chenoweth, hearing
a suspicious noise about his door, sprang from his bed and
seized his rifle, but as he was advancing toward his door
was shot down by an Indian. His wife immediately took up
her husband's gun and shot the Indian dead; and then pick-
ing up an ax, flew to the door, and as the Indians attempted
to force their way in she killed two more with the ax; a
fourth jumped on her cabin and was making his way down
the chimney, but she threw an old bed, or something of the
kind, on the fire, smoked him down, and killed him also.
The fifth Indian now ran away, and she had leisure to attend
to her husband, who was not mortally wounded. She dressed
his wounds, and he finally recovered. I had this story from
the man himself, who appeared to be a man of plain manners,
and I had no reason to doubt his veracity. But it was many
years ago, and I may be mistaken in some particulars in the
detail; it is, however, I believe, substantially correct; and if
so, which of you, my fair countrywomen, at this day could
do likewise? The story of the two little fellows of the name
of Johnson, who killed two Indian men who had taken them
prisoners, is of more recent date, and I believe is so generally known that it need not be repeated here.

The reader, may, perhaps, be of opinion this chapter has no
immediate connection with the subject matter before us. That
it has not that immediate connection, we allow; but as Captain Cresap was now in his zenith, and a conspicuous character
at this period, and among the first and most valuable officers
in the Revolutionary War, it was thought a general view of
the state of the Nation might tend to illustrate and shed light
upon our history, and therefore serve as a proper introduction
before we present him personally to public view—more especially as this war cost him his life.

CHAPTER II.

The Cresap Family.

The author is aware that a mere catalogue of names, however respectable, must be an insipid and tasteless treat to the reader; but in the present case it seems so indispensable that if omitted it would leave a chasm in his book, so all-important as to supersede in a good degree the necessity of this work; because it is evident that, inasmuch as Captain Cresap is now dead, and so long dead, if his accusers and enemies had suffered his ashes to rest in peace, time itself, at this late day, would have nearly obliterated the memory of his name.* But, I say, as Captain Cresap is now dead and beyond the reach of malevolence and calumny, so of course nothing that has been or can be said can affect him personally. But the Cresap family is large, extensive and respectable; it will not yield the homage of superiority to any family in Virginia or Maryland. If, then, those black spots—this stigma upon the name and character of Captain Cresap—were permitted to remain, it would affect the whole family through all its various branches to the remotest degree of affinity. Hence the necessity of presenting to public view all or most of the names and grades of a family thus attempted to be exposed to public infamy.

Colonel Thomas Cresap, the father of the subject of this memoir, and the head and founder of the Cresap family,

---

* Dr. D. tells us in his preface that a pious regard for the ashes of ancestors is not without its influence on the morals and piety of their descendants. If this be true, what shall we say of those who labor to consign those ashes to infamy and abhorrence?

emigrated from Yorkshire, England, when about fifteen
years of age; but the dark shades of oblivion rest upon all
the intermediate part of his life from this period until he
arrived at the age of about thirty, when he married a Miss
Johnson, and settled at or near the place now called Havre-
de-Grace, on the Susquehanna. He was at this time poor,
and in providing the necessary articles for housekeeping got
involved in debt to the enormous sum of nine pounds, currency, when, with a view it is believed to extricate himself
from the pressure of this debt, he took a trip to Virginia,
got acquainted with and rented a farm from the Washington
family, with the intention of removing to that colony. But
during his absence his wife was delivered of her first-born
son, Daniel, and on his return refused to go with him to
Virginia. Now, however he might be displeased at this, he
acquiesced; and after having paid his nine pound debt he
removed higher up the Susquehanna, to or near the place
called Wright's Ferry, opposite where the town of Columbia
now stands, and obtained a Maryland title for five hundred
acres of good land. But this, unfortunately, at that time was
disputed territory; and as others set up a claim to this
land under a Pennsylvania title, a war—called the Conojacular war—took place. Cresap espoused the cause of Lord
Baltimore with as much zeal and ardor as the Pennites did
that of Mr. Penn; and a battle ensued at a place called
Peach Bottom. Cresap's party proved victorious, kept the
field, and wounded some of the Pennites. But they soon
recruited their army and besieged the old fellow in his own
house—which happened, I think, to be built of stone. The
attack was made in the night; but as the besiegers had
neither cannon nor battering rams, it was found that the
fort was impregnable. Finding that it would in all proba-

bility be a work of time, the besiegers built a fire some distance from the house, that they might warm themselves, counsel and deliberate. Cresap, aware of his perilous situation, put out his son Daniel, now nine or ten years old, to warn his neighbors and friends to his assistance; but the assailants discovered and took him prisoner. The little fellow, however, well nigh played them a trick, for, seeing their powder in a handkerchief, he seized and attempted to throw it into the fire, which he certainly would have done, but they saw and prevented it.

The besiegers, finding all their efforts unavailing, at length adopted the same plan that Colonel Lee devised to take the British in Mrs. Mott's new house in Carolina, during our Revolutionary War—namely, setting fire to the roof of his house. This had the desired effect, and the fort was no longer tenable. As no terms of capitulation were offered, the Colonel flew to the door, wounding the sentinel who stood there, and made good his retreat to his boat, which happened to be so fast as not to be loosened in time, and he was surrounded and taken. They tied his hands behind him, and were pushing across the river with their herculean prisoner watched and guarded by a man on each side; but our old Yorkshire hero, seizing a favorable opportunity, elbowed one of his guard overboard into the river. The night being dark, the Pennites thought it was Cresap in the water, and fell upon him randum tandum with their poles; but poor Paddy—he was an Irishman—not pleased at all at all with this sport, made such lamentable cries that, discovering their mistake, they hoisted him out of his cold bath.

When the guard arrived at Lancaster with the prisoner they had him handcuffed with iron, which was no sooner done than, raising both hands together, he gave the smith such a tremendous blow upon his black pate that it brought him to the ground. Now, having their prisoner secure, they marched him in triumph to the city of Philadelphia, where the streets, windows and doors were crowded with spectators to view such a monster of a man. He, the more to irritate them, exclaimed, "Why, this is the finest city in the State of Maryland!" And indeed it appears that he really thought so. I have myself more than once heard him say that if Lord Baltimore had attended to his own interests, or regarded his own rights, his title to the city of Philadelphia was certainly good; for inasmuch as the charter of the State of Maryland extended to the 40th degree of north latitude, it included the whole of that degree, and was not to be limited by the beginning.

But to resume our history. After the party reached Philadelphia with their prisoner he was committed to jail; but for some reasons not recollected it seems they soon grew weary of their guest and wanted him to go home, which he refused to do until liberated, I believe by order of the King. During all the time of the colonel's captivity Mrs. Cresap, with her children, took shelter in an Indian town on Condorus, near Little York, where they were received and hospitably supported by the Indians until he returned to his family. Soon after this Colonel Cresap removed to Antietam, on a valuable farm called the Long Meadows, now in possession of the Sprigg family. On this farm he built a house of stone over a spring, designed as a fort, because he was on the frontier and in advance of a white population. He now commenced as an Indian trader, and borrowed from Mr. Dulany £500, to aid him in his business. Having provided a large quantity of skins and furs, he shipped them for England. But fortune still frowned. The ship was taken by the French, with all his skins and furs, and once more he was compelled to begin the world anew. In this dilemma he sent for Mr. Dulany, stated his loss, and offered him his land—about 1,400 acres—for the debt. Mr. Dulany acceded to the proposal, and Colonel Cresap made another remove, to the place now called Old Town, but by himself called Skipton, after the place of his nativity. This place is a few miles above the junction of the North and South branches of the Potomac, on the North fork, and at length became the place of his permanent residence; and here he acquired an immense landed estate on both sides of the river—*i. e.*, in Virginia and Maryland. It was, perhaps, about this time, or soon after, that, having renewed his acquaintance with the Washington family, he entered conjointly into an association with two or three gentlemen of this name—of whom, I think, the General was one—Colonel George Mason, and many other gentlemen in England and America, and formed what was called "The Ohio Company." This Company made the first English settlement at Pittsburg before Braddock's war; and it was through their means and efforts that the first path was traced through that vast chain of mountains called the Allegheny. Colonel Cresap, as one of that Company, and active agent thereof in this section of the country, employed an honest and friendly Indian to lay out and mark a road from Cumberland to Pittsburg. This Indian's name was Nemacolin; and he did his work so well that General Braddock with his army pursued the same path, which thenceforward took the name of Braddock's road, and which does not at this day materially differ from the present great National Road.

There can be no doubt that the exertions and influence of this Company had a strong tendency to accelerate the exploration and settlement of the Western country. They were, in fact, and might truly be said to be the corps of Pioneers that opened the way to that immense flood of population we now see spreading like a mighty torrent to the Pacific Ocean; and it may not, perhaps, be amiss at this place to state a circumstance, perfectly in my memory, demonstrative of that energetic and enterprising spirit always so conspicuous in the character of Colonel Cresap. The circumstance I allude to is a plan conceived and digested by the old gentleman when, I believe, upward of ninety years of age; it was to explore and examine the country quite to the Western ocean, and it appeared so rational and practicable, that if he had been thirty years younger it is probable he would himself have tested its practicability.

But to return. We do not pretend to say that all those efforts and exertions of the Ohio Company were purely disinterested. Not so; nor would it be reasonable to expect it. On the contrary, they felt the impulse of a strong excitement from a most powerful motive, viz: self-interest. They had the promise from the King and court of Great Britain of a grant for 500,000 acres of land on the Ohio, and this land was actually surveyed in 1775, but our Revolution prevented the consummation of the title. But let their motive be what it might, the Nation, it must be acknowledged, is under obligations to this Company, and especially to the bold and enterprising spirit of *Colonel Cresap for an early knowledge and acquisition of the country west of the Allegheny mountains.

But there is a very material fact not to be forgotten in the annals of our history, to-wit: that soon after the settlement made at Pittsburg, under the auspices and at the expense of the Ohio Company, the place was taken possession of by the

---

* I have among my papers a bill paid by Colonel Cresap to an old fellow for digging Sideling Hill, amounting to £25.

French, who built a Fort, and which they called Duquesne. This place being considered all-important as well by England as by France, soon became a bone of contention; a war ensued, which cost England two hot-headed Scotch Generals, Braddock and Grant—the latter I believe was only a colonel —and their armies many subsequent battles and much blood and treasure to regain possession of this place, and it is possible, I think, that the great battle between Wolf and Montcalm on the plains of Abraham, near Quebec, decided the fate of the whole Western country.

This war, which is known and distinguished in this country by the term of *Braddock's War*, placed Colonel Cresap and his family in a perilous situation. The settlers around him were few and thinly scattered, and the settlement in fact was broken up. Colonel Cresap removed his family to Conococheague, but he was compelled to fight his way, for he had advanced but five or six miles on his journey when he was attacked by some Indians. They did no injury, however, and were soon dispersed—after which he proceeded without further molestation.

It appears, however, that he did not remain an idle spectator of these scenes of blood and devastation that threatened ruin and desolation to the infant settlements on the head of the Potomac. He raised a company of volunteers, and marched to attack his Indian enemies whenever and wherever he might find them. He pursued, it seems, Braddock's road, not expecting, it is probable, to meet with the enemy until he had crossed the mountains; but if so, he was deceived, for he met a small party of Indians just on the west foot of the Savage mountain; a battle ensued, and his son Thomas was killed by an Indian; but as both fired at the same time, he also killed the Indian, or so badly wounded him that he was killed a few minutes afterward by William Lynn. Nothing more, I believe, was done at this time or place, and the party returned home.

Colonel Cresap, however, soon got together another company of volunteers, and with his two surviving sons—Daniel and Michael—and a negro of gigantic stature, marched again, taking the same route on Braddock's road. They advanced this time as far as Negro mountain, where they met a party of Indians. A running fight took place; Cresap's party killed an Indian and the Indians killed the negro; and it was this circumstance—the death of the negro on the mountain—that has immortalized his name by fixing it on this ridge forever. This was, I believe, Colonel Cresap's last battle with the Indians, for after peace was made, he returned to his farm at Old Town, and what I have further to say respecting Colonel Cresap will be rather in the disjunctive and desultory way.

The reader has not forgotten, perhaps, that I have already mentioned the name of the Indian Nemacolin, employed by Colonel Cresap to lay out the road to Pittsburg. Now so strong was the affection of this Indian for Colonel Cresap and his family, that he not only spent much of his time with them, but before he finally went away, brought his son George and left him with the family to raise; and it is a fact within my own knowledge that this George lived and died in the family.

Again, at the time of Colonel Cresap's Conojacular war with the Pennites, they hired an Indian to go to his house and kill him. The Indian accordingly went to the Colonel's house, and continued lounging about several days, reluctant savage as he was to commit such cold blooded murder, until at length overcome with the kindness of the family, he confessed the whole, and went away in peace.

Once more, while the Indians were carrying on the desolating war already noticed upon the head waters of the Potomac, and other frontier settlements, they one day made an attack upon Colonel Cresap's fort, at his own house, near Old Town. They killed a Mr. Wilder,* who happened to be some distance from the fort; but the attack was feeble, easily repelled, and the Indian was killed who killed Mr. Wilder. But a certain old Indian named Kill-buck contrived to get under a bridge over a mill race, about one hundred and fifty yards from the fort, where he lay quietly and patiently, two or three days and nights, with the sole view of killing old Cresap, whom he never saw during the whole time; and to add to his mortification, one day, while lying under the bridge, an old woman coming on the bridge, stopped directly over him, and let her water upon him. Now, whether this old fellow had ever heard of the Philosopher Socrates and his wife Xantippe, I know not; but certain it is, that under similar circumstances he was more passive and silent than even Socrates himself. For this story we are indebted to Kill-buck himself, or it would have remained a secret forever.

Although we believe every man is under the protection of Providence, yet from these anecdotes it would seem to appear.

---

* As Mr. Saml. Wilder was going to a house of his about 300 yards Distant from mine with 4 men and several women, the Indians rushed on them from a rising Ground, but they perceving them coming, Run towards my house hollowing, which being heard by those at my house, they run to their assistance and met them and tne Indians at the Entrance of my lane, on which the Indians Immdiately fired on them to the amount of 18 or Twenty and Killed Mr. Wilder,—the party of white men Returned their fire and killed one of them dead on the Spot and wounded severall of the others as appeared by Considerable Quantity of Blood strewed on the Ground as they Run off, which they Immdiately did, and by their leaving behind them 3 Gunns, one pistole and Sundry other Emplements of warr &c. &c.
I have Inclosed a List of the Desolate men, Women and Children who have fled to my house which is Inclosed by a small stockade for safety, by which you'll see what a number of poor Souls, destitute of Every neccessary of Life are here penned up and likely to be Butchered without Immdiate Relief and assistance, and cad Expect none, unless from the province to which they Belong. I shall submitt to your wiser Judgment the Best and most Effectual method for Such Relief, and shall Conclude with hoping we shall have it in time.— *Extract from a Letter from Colonel Thomas Cresap to Governor Sharpe, of Maryland.*

that this old gentleman was most specially and peculiarly preserved.

Colonel Cresap's literary attainments were small; the incidents and unpropitious circumstances of his early life were such as to preclude and forbid every thing of this nature. His mind was, however, vigorous, comprehensive and strong; for notwithstanding the defect in his early education, and all the disadvantage of acquiring scientific knowledge in mature age, yet by industry and application he obtained a sufficient knowledge of mathematics to be entrusted with the surveyorship of Prince George's county;* and such also was his decision and energy of mind, that he frequently represented his county in the Legislature, and for clearness of understanding, soundness of judgment, and firmness of mind, he was esteemed one of the best members.

Perhaps no part of Colonel Cresap's character was more estimated than his benevolence and hospitality. In early times when there were but few taverns, and those few were very indifferent, his house at Old Town was open and his table spread for all decent travelers, and they were welcome. His delight was to give and receive useful information; nor was this friendly disposition limited to white people only. The Indians generally called on him in pretty large parties as they passed and repassed from North to South on their war expeditions, and for which special purpose he kept a very large kettle for their use; and he also generally gave them a beef to kill for themselves every time they called, and his liberality toward them gained for him among them the honorable title of the *Big-spoon*.

His person was not large but firmly set, and his muscular strength was very great; he had a sound constitution,

---

* This county at that time comprehended Montgomery, Frederick, Washington and Allegheny.

and lived to the uncommon age of one hundred and five or six. About the age of three score and ten he undertook and performed a voyage to England, and came back in safety, bringing with him four nieces—sister's daughters*—one of whom, an ancient woman, is still living. While in London, Colonel Cresap was commissioned by Lord Baltimore to run the western line of Maryland, with a view to ascertain which of the two branches of the Potomac was the largest, and which was in reality the fountain-head or first source of that river.† I recollect having heard Colonel Cresap say that many years ago some gentlemen who were appointed commissioners to settle this question, came up to the junction of the two branches, but considering it difficult and dangerous to proceed further, measured the width and depth of the rivers, and finding the north branch the widest and deepest, reported accordingly.

On his return home he employed surveyors and run the line, as follows: A due north line from the head spring of the north branch to intersect the Pennsylvania line, and then beginning at the head spring of the south branch and running a parallel line north to the Pennsylvania line. It was thus discovered that the line from the head of the south branch was twelve miles west of that drawn from the north branch; hence it is probable that if our Revolution had not dissolved the charter of Baltimore and Fairfax, that the high Court

---

* I am aware that public report has attached a different and unfavorable character to these women, but they were really his nieces. Three of them married, and one returned to England.

† The original autograph map was made by Colonel Cresap, in the neat style of a good country surveyor, and sent by him to Governor Sharpe. It came to Mr. Gilmor's possession with many other of the "Ridout Papers," and is attested by Horatio Ridout, whose father was Sharpe's secretary. This was the *first* map ever made to show the course and fountains of the north and south branches of the Potomac river, in regard to which there has been so much controversy between Maryland and Virginia.—*Gilmor MSS., Maryland Papers, vol.* 1, *Portfolio of "Surveys, Letters, etc., connected with the running of the Division line between Maryland and Pennsylvania."*

4

of Chancery in Great Britain would have had an important cause to decide; but as the case now stands, it is a question between the two States of Maryland and Virginia, which may, it is possible, in some future day become a subject of inquiry and investigation.

A few more remarks and I am done with Colonel Cresap. When he was upward of eighty years old he married a second wife, and at the age of about one hundred, performed a journey, partly by sea and partly by land, from his residence at Old Town to an island near the British Province of Nova Scotia, and returned in safety. From this we seem warranted in asserting, that had Providence—or chance if you like the word better—placed Colonel Cresap at the head of an army, or state, or kingdom, he would have been a more conspicuous character. He was not inferior to Charles XII of Sweden in personal bravery; nor to Peter the Great of Russia—whom in many things he much resembled—in coolness and fortitude, or that peculiar talent of learning experience from misfortune, and levying a tax upon damage and loss to raise him to future prosperity and success.

Having now done with Colonel Cresap, I must entreat the reader's patience while I enter with some minuteness upon a catalogue of the Cresap family. I have already assigned— and need not repeat them—weighty reasons for pursuing this course.

Colonel Thomas Cresap had five children; three sons—Daniel, Thomas and Michael; and two daughters—Sarah and Elizabeth.

Daniel was a plain man—the patriarch of the day and country in which he lived—a man of sober habits, great industry, economy and temperance. Like Jacob of old, agriculture was his occupation and delight; and in the midst of his family, his flocks, and his herds, he spent his days and acquired immense wealth. He was proverbially the poor man's friend, and has been known, in scarce times, to refuse to sell corn to those who had money, that he might have enough to supply those who had none; and I suspect this original, although faithful portrait, has but few copies. What a pity.

I do not purpose writing the lives of all the Cresaps, yet there are a few circumstances in this man's life that deserve recording, especially as they have a remote bearing on the main object of this work, namely: to show that the public are greatly deceived in their opinion of the Cresap family respecting Indians and Indian affairs.

Old Nemacolin, the Indian already mentioned, was very intimate with and spent much of his time in the family of Daniel Cresap. They agreed one day to go out on a bear hunt, and after getting into what they thought proper ground, they separated, having fixed upon a place known to both where they would meet. Cresap pursued his way to the top of the Allegheny mountain, and soon started and treed some cubs. Anxious to get the cubs, and to learn his dog to fight them, he ascended the tree; but the cubs still moving higher, he pursued until the limbs of the tree broke, and down came Cresap and cubs to the ground—or rather to the stones—for it happened on a rough, stony piece of ground. This fall from such a height, and among stones, broke his bones, and nearly took his life. He lay on the ground motionless and senseless until the old Indian, who not finding him at the time and place agreed upon, and supposing that something had befallen him, had the good fortune to find him, after diligent search, in the situation above described; but his wounds and bruises were such that he could not be moved. Nemacolin, moved with compassion, went to his house and informed his wife, and between them with the aid of a horse and litter they took him to his home.

I tell the reader this story not only to show the habits of intimacy between the Cresap family and the Indians, but it was this circumstance—or his dwelling in the vicinity of the mountain—that has immortalized his name ; for it was from him that the ridge of the Allegheny mountain called Dan's Mountain took its name, and which I presume is fixed on it forever.

Daniel Cresap—son of Colonel Thomas—had by his first wife one son, Michael, who commanded a company in Dunmore's war, and was afterward colonel of the militia of Hampshire County, Virginia, who is dead ; and by a second wife he had seven sons and three daughters, to-wit : Thomas, Daniel, Joseph, Van, Robert, James, and Thomas again; and Elizabeth, Mary and Sarah. Thomas died young.

Daniel Cresap—son of Daniel—was a lieutenant in his uncle Michael's company of Riflemen, who marched to Boston in 1775 ; was afterward colonel of the militia of Allegheny county, Maryland, and also commanded a regiment in General Lee's army against the whisky boys. He died on his return from this expedition.

Joseph, his second son by his second wife, was also with his uncle in Dunmore's war, although very young. He was in both expeditions : that commanded by McDonald, and also in that commanded by Dunmore in person. He also marched to Boston in the company commanded by his uncle, and was one of his lieutenants. He has often represented the county of Allegheny, Maryland, in the Legislature, and was lastly a member of the Senate. He is still living, is a man of wealth and respectability, has been four times married, and has a large family of children.

Van, his fourth son, is dead. He left two sons and two daughters, three of whom are still living, have families, and are respectable.

Robert, like his father, is a plain, domestic man. His habits of industry and economy have produced their natural results—wealth and independence—and in respect to wealth, is among the first in Allegheny county. He is yet living, and has a large family of children.

James is rich and very popular; has often represented his county in the State Legislature, and has a fine family of children. He is still living.

Thomas, his youngest son, occupies his father's old mansion house, and is highly respectable; has also represented his county in the State Legislature; is at present one of the judges of the Orphan's Court; is living, and has a large family of children.

And now may I not ask: how many fathers have so many sons honorable to their family and in such high estimation among their fellow citizens?

Elizabeth, his eldest daughter, was married to Thomas Collins, Esq., of Hampshire county, Virginia. They are both dead, but left several children, one of whom is—or was—colonel of the militia of Hampshire, but he has removed to Maryland.

Mary, his second daughter, was unfortunate in her marriage, but her dissipated husband is dead, and she has several fine children.

Sarah, his youngest daughter, is married to Aquilla A. Brown, Esq., attorney at law; they reside in Philadelphia, are wealthy and respectable, and have several fine children.

Thomas Cresap—second son of Colonel Thomas—was, as already related, killed by an Indian, but both firing at the same instant, killed each other. He was married and left a widow and one female child. This daughter of Thomas Cresap, Jr., was first married to a Mr. Brent, a lawyer, by whom she had a son and daughter, both still living. Her son Thomas Brent, Esq., lives in Washington county, Maryland, and is wealthy and respectable. She was afterward married to John Reid, Esq., of Allegheny county; they had several children, one of which, William Reid, Esq., is now a representative for his county.

Michael Cresap, the subject of this memoir and youngest son of Colonel Thomas, left five children—two sons and three daughters. But as the daughters were the oldest we will begin with them:

Mary, the eldest daughter, was married to Luther Martin, Esq., Attorney General of Maryland. She is dead, and has left two daughters, one of whom is also dead.

Elizabeth, the second daughter, married Lenox Martin, Esq.,—brother of Luther. He was also raised to the profession of the law, and was for a period a practitioner, but is now a justice of the peace, and resides in Allegheny county, near Old Town. Himself and wife are both living, and have a large family of children.

Sarah, the youngest daughter, married Osborn Sprigg, Esq. They are both dead, but left four sons, one of whom (Michael) is a popular character, and at present is a candidate for Congress with a fair prospect of success.

James, the eldest son, was first married to a Miss Reid, but she dying young, he afterward married Mrs. Vanbiber, widow of Mr. Abraham Vanbiber, of Baltimore, by whom he had one son, Luther Martin Cresap, who is still living, but his father is dead.

Michael, youngest son of Captain Michael, married a Miss

Ogle, a young lady raised by his mother. They live on the Ohio river, have several fine children, and are wealthy and respectable.

Sarah, daughter of Colonel Thomas Cresap, was twice married; first to Colonel Enoch Innis, and afterward to a Mr. John Foster. They are all dead, and she had no children.

Elizabeth, the youngest daughter of Colonel Thomas Cresap, was married to a Mr. Isaac Collier, from Pennsylvania, who was rather a dissipated character. They are both dead, but left several children, who reside in the States of Kentucky, Ohio and Alabama, and all of them are wealthy and respectable.

Thus have I brought into public view this numerous and respectable family, that it may at once be seen how many persons and characters of the first estimation, who move in the highest circles of society wherever they dwell, and who certainly—in a comparative view—stand upon equal ground with any family of the United States; and where, permit me to add, shall we find a catalogue of names, all of the same stock and family, so free from blemishes and so equally and generally respectable. I regret that there should be any exceptions, but they are few. And shall I, who know them all, and know that the charges against one of the most conspicuous characters of this family are most untrue; knowing, I say, as I do, that Captain Michael Cresap was neither a man infamous for his many Indian murders nor the cause of Dunmore's war—with this conviction upon my mind, with the truth before me as clear as the resplendent beams of the sun —shall I, or can I, remain silent when I have it in my power most positively and completely to refute all these charges? Surely I shall be pardoned if, contrary to my wish or intention, any warmth or disrespectful expression toward Captain Cresap's accuser should unguardedly drop from my pen, for I verily believe few circumstances in life can have a stronger tendency to irritation and warmth of excitement than to be contradicted, browbeaten and pertinaciously opposed as to the truth of a well known fact, especially in all cases where the character of a friend is calumniated, and, contrary to truth and reason, is consigned, or attempted to be consigned, to public execration and infamy.

If indeed Captain Cresap was the man represented by Mr. Jefferson—*infamous for his many Indian murders*—or if as Mr. Doddridge, of recent date, asserts, *he was the cause of Dunmore's war*, the public would never have heard from me. I should neither have stained paper nor opened my mouth. But conscious as I am that there is not a word of truth in all this, I stand upon *terra firma*; I set my feet upon this immutable basis of truth, stretch out my hand and defy the world! I am no Cresap; his widow, it is true, was my wife, and he was my friend; my more than friend—my foster father. The world will therefore judge how far I should be excusable were I to remain silent in a cause so just, in a case so clear. Nay! like one of old, we say: "*We cannot but speak of the things we have seen and heard.*"

CHAPTER III.

A brief sketch of the life of Captain Cresap's youth up to the year 1774.

It is not my view in this work to give the public a detailed or particular history of the life of Captain Cresap, but only so much and such parts as is deemed necessary to present his life as a whole portrait sufficiently united in symmetry—to present in full view a character not known, but little understood though much abused by those who judge without knowledge and condemn without reason.

He was, as has been already stated, the youngest son of Colonel Thomas Cresap, of Frederick—but now Allegheny —county, Maryland, and was born on the 29th day of June, 1742. The remoteness of Colonel Cresap's habitation from a dense population, or any seminary of learning, induced the old gentleman to send his son Michael to a school in Baltimore county, kept by the Rev. Mr. Craddock; but young Cresap being a backwoods boy, and speckled bird among his school fellows, had to fight his way into their good graces, which, I think, he soon effected, and became their champion. Not relishing, however, the restraints of a school, or for some other cause, he ran away, and traveled home on foot, a distance of 140 miles. But his father, far from sanctioning any such conduct, gave the poor fellow a terrible whipping and sent him back, where thenceforward he steadily remained until he had finished his education; soon after which he married a Miss Whitehead, of Philadelphia—both very young—and settling in a little village near his father's residence, commenced life as a merchant. He imported his goods first from London, dealt largely, and well nigh ruined himself from his benevolence and misplaced confidence in his customers. A circumstance also occurred about this time that injured him most materially. The gentleman who acted as agent for the London merchant from whom he received his goods, wrote to him that Cresap was a suspicious character, and that he was under the apprehension he intended to remove to some place in the Western country where he would be out of the reach of the law. But this story came to the ears of Captain Cresap; his goods were withheld and the cause discovered. The consequence was that a dreadful battle ensued between Cresap and this agent, whose name I forbear to mention. This dreadful battle was fought in a private room in Fredericktown, and I am under the impression that no other person was present. But Captain Cresap soon discovered that fighting did not fill his coffers, and however other men—as Cyrus, Alexander and Napoleon—might amass wealth and treasure from the science of war and man-killing, yet it had an inverse operation on his funds, as will appear in the sequel of his history.

But to return from this digression. Captain Cresap, from the causes above recited, discovered that his affairs were in a ruinous condition, and might be said to be daily growing worse. From the peculiar circumstances of the times, the tide of emigration began to flow with great rapidity to the West, and his debtors, some to a large amount, were daily removing to the land of milk and honey. He now discovered that he had dealt upon too liberal a scale, and though late, determined to be more cautious in the future. I was in his store at this time, and was strictly charged by him to trust no man unless I knew him to be good; but if at any time he was caught in the store him-self—which sometimes happened—a plausible story from a man, or a piteous tale from a woman, would soon demolish all the fortifications about his heart; and the result was, turning to me, he would say: John, let this man or this woman have what they want! and soon after leave the store for fear of another attack.

Captain Cresap's whole deportment, in all his various relations, diversified scenes and circumstances, exhibited the character of a benevolent, noble and generous spirit. He was a man of uncommon energy, enterprise and decision—plan and execution with him followed in rapid succession, and as already remarked, the deranged and unpropitious aspect of his affairs determined him to adopt some judi-cious and feasible plan to rescue his sinking fortune from ruin. The case admitted of no parley or delay; nor was his character of a complexion to hesitate. He saw a way open, and that way he boldly pursued, conscious that he must emerge from the ocean of difficulty in which he was involved or sink. Thus urged by necessity—prompted by a laudable ambition and allured by the rational and exhil-arating prospect before him—he thought he saw in the rich bottoms of the Ohio an ample fund if he succeeded in se-curing a title to those lands, not only to redeem his credit and extricate himself from his difficulty, but also to afford a respectable competency for a rising family.

Under the impression of this idea, and with every rational prospect of success, early in the Spring of the year 1774, he engaged six or seven active young men, under the wages of £2 10s 0d, each per month, and repairing to the then wilderness of the Ohio, commenced the business of building houses and clearing lands; and being one of the first adventurers into this exposed and dangerous region, he had it in his power to select some of the best and richest of the Ohio bottoms. But, while thus peaceably and diligently engaged in the prosecution of his object, he was suddenly arrested by a circular letter from Major Connoly, the Earl of Dunmore's Vice-Governor of Western Virginia, and commandant at Pittsburg. This letter was sent by express in every direction through the country, warning the inhabitants to be on their guard; that the Indians were very angry and manifested such a hostile disposition that it was evident they would fall on the inhabitants somewhere. As soon as the season would permit, this letter was sent to Captain Cresap, accompanied with a confirmatory message from Colonel Croghan and Alexander M'Gee, Esq., Indian agents and interpreters. The result was, that Captain Cresap immediately abandoned his object, and ascended the Ohio to Fort Wheeling, the nearest place of safety.

As I shall give the reader a more ample detail of the whole affair in my next chapter, I shall waive any further remarks at this time, save only that from the foregoing statement, which I am confident is substantially correct, it is most apparent that Captain Cresap's primary, yea, only object in leaving his family and stationing himself on the banks of the Ohio, in the Spring of the year 1774, was to secure and improve some lands on that river; and consequently, that an Indian war would be to him, above all men, most disastrous, and therefore to be deprecated and dreaded as opposed to all his golden dreams of ease and affluence in declining life—and this single circumstance will serve as a key to all subsequent facts, and tend to open and elucidate the natural results, causes and effects, as it should seem inevitably growing out of this state of things at this period.

Captain Cresap's loss and sacrifice on this occasion, affords an auxiliary and powerful argument in support of what is remarked above; for in addition to the paralyzing and blasted views now presented to his mind respecting his own lands, his expenses must have amounted to nearly £30 per month—adding subsistence, at such a distance from any place where provisions could be obtained—to the monthly wages of his men. He had also with him the necessary furniture and camp equipage, which he foresaw must be, and I believe was, finally lost.

May I not then be permitted to repeat, that it must be evident that no man of sane mind—that none but a madman—could under these circumstances, at this time, have wished for an Indian war.

CHAPTER IV

Dunmore's war—preliminary remarks—inquiry into the cause—
Connoly's circular letter—state of the Western country in
the year 1774*—Captain Cresap improving lands—ascent*
to Fort Wheeling—two Indians killed in a canoe—subse-
quent affair with the Indians—skirmish on the Ohio—
quarrel with Connoly, and return to his family—Commis-
sion from and implied approbation of the Earl of Dunmore
—Major McDonald's expedition to Wappatomica—Dun-
more's campaign—Treaty at Chillicothe—conclusion of the
war.

It will appear from the bill of fare, or short analysis of
the various subjects embraced in the chapter before us,
that we are now entering into an extensive field; a field
so fraught with important matter, that it will require the
closest attention, and utmost accuracy to delineate in their
true colors the various and multifarious scenes through which
we are destined to travel; and inasmuch as what I am now
about to detail may become matter of record to succeeding
ages, I cannot but feel an uncommon solicitude to keep close
in the straight path of truth, and therefore, it is my design,
while I speak positively as to known facts, to be cautious and
guarded in my expressions as to doubtful subjects.

And permit me to add that I am now old, and as all the
facts and circumstances I am now about to record, are also old
—obsolete, and to most men of this generation unknown, and
I believe nearly obliterated from the memory of my co-equals

in age—neither is my memory very tenacious ; it is therefore possible I may be mistaken in the detail of some trivial circumstances, and I now promise, that if a reader should discover any such mistake of sufficient importance to merit correction, I will then freely do it—provided he is right and I am wrong.

The question of justice, or injustice, as to the means used by the American nation in the acquisition of the Indians' lands, and their gradual expulsion from their native seats, farther and still farther West, I leave to be settled among statesmen and philosophers, who have more leisure and better talents for the discussion ; but it is certain that our quarrel with the Indians, or their quarrel with us, is nearly coeval with our earliest settlement on this continent. It is true that we have had many treaties, and often made peace, with our aboriginal neighbors, but this state of things was never permanent. The restless, roving disposition of the Indians, whose only business is hunting and war, together with the frequent encroachments of the white people on their lands and hunting grounds, soon kindled again the fire-brands of war, which was generally protracted and destructive in its effects in proportion to the number of Indian nations engaged, and their aggregate numerical strength.

At this period, to-wit : in the commencement of the year 1774, there existed between our people and the Indians, a kind of doubtful, precarious and suspicious peace. In the year 1773, they killed a certain John Martin and Guy Meeks, (Indian traders), on the Hockhocking, and robbed them of about £200 worth of goods. They were much irritated with our people, who were about this time settling Kentucky, and with them they waged an unceasing and destructive predatory war ; and whoever saw an Indian in Kentucky saw an enemy

LEARNING RESOURCES CENTER
NAZARETH COLLEGE

—no questions were asked on either side but from the muzzles of their rifles. Many other circumstances at this period combined to show that our peace with the Indians rested upon such dubious and uncertain ground, that it must soon be dispersed by a whirlwind of war and carnage, and as I consider this an all-important point in the thread of our history, and an interesting link in the chain of causes combining to produce Dunmore's war, I will present the reader with another fact directly in point; it is extracted from the journal of Esquire M'Connel, in my possession. Esquire M'Connel says, that about the 3d day of March, 1774, while himself and six other men, who were in company with him, were asleep in their camp in the night, they were awakened by the fierce barking of their dogs, and thought they saw something like men creeping toward them. Alarmed at this, they sprang up, seized their rifles and flew to trees. By this time one Indian had reached their fire, but hearing them cock their guns, drew back, stumbled and fell. The whole party now came up, and appearing friendly, he ordered his men not to fire, and shook hands with his new guests. They tarried all night, and appeared so friendly, prevailed with him and one of his men to go with them to their town, at no great distance from their camp; but when they arrived, he was taken with his companion to their council—or war house—a war dance was performed around them, and the war club shook at, or over, them, and they were detained close prisoners and narrowly guarded for two or three days. A council was held over them, and it was decreed that they should be threatened severely and discharged, provided they would give their women some flour and salt. Being dismissed, they set out on their journey to their camp, but met on their way about twenty-five warriors and some boys; a second council was held over them, and it was decreed that they should not be killed, but robbed, which was accordingly done, and all their flour, salt, powder and lead, and all their rifles that were good, were taken from them; and being further threatened, the Indians left them. As already noticed, this party consisted of seven men, to-wit: Esquire M'Connel, Andrew M'Connel, Lawrence Darnal, William Ganet, Matthew Riddle, John Laferty, and Thomas Canady.

But I must advertise the reader here, that I have condensed, and not copied verbatim, Esquire M'Connel's journal —it was too long to transcribe.*

We have also in reserve some material facts, that go to show the aspect of affairs at this period, and that may be considered as evident precursors to an impending war. And it is certainly not a trifling item in the catalogue of these events, that early in the Spring of 1774—whether precedent or subsequent to Connoly's famous circular letter I am not prepared to say, having no positive data; but it was, however, about this period—that the Indians killed two men in a canoe, belonging to a Mr. Butler,† of Pittsburg, and robbed the canoe of the property therein. This was about the first of May, 1774, and took place near the mouth of Little Beaver, a small creek that empties into the Ohio between Pittsburg and Wheeling—and this fact is so certain and well established,

---

* Since writing this chapter, Mr. Joseph Cresap stated to me this fact, evincing the general impression on the minds of the western people of an immediate attack from the Indians. He says that in the month of April, in the year 1774, he was with some surveyors running lands on Cheat river, about four miles above the Horse-shoe bottom; that they were indistinctly discovered by some hunters who reported that they were a party of Indians; that a company was immediately raised in Tyger's Valley, who marched down about thirty miles to attack them, but fortunately discovered their mistake before any mischief was done.

† Mr. William Butler, who seems not to have heeded the earlier warnings, had sent off a canoe, loaded with goods for the Shawanese towns, and on the 16th of April it was attacked, forty miles below Pittsburg, by three Cherokees, who waylaid it on the river. They killed one white man, wounded another, while a third made his escape, and the savages plundered the canoe of the most valuable part of the cargo.—*Discourse by Brantz Mayer, delivered before the Maryland Historical Society, p. 48.*

that Benjamin Tomlinson, Esq.,—who is now living, and assisted in burying the dead—can, and will, bear testimony to its truth.

And, it is presumed, it was this circumstance that produced that prompt and terrible vengeance, taken on the Indians at Yellow Creek immediately after, to-wit: on the 3d of May, which gave rise to, and furnished matter for, the pretended lying speech of Logan, which I shall hereafter prove a counterfeit; and if it was genuine, yet a genuine fabrication of lies.

Thus we find from an examination into the state of affairs in the West, that there was a pre-disposition to war at least on the part of the Indians. But may we not suspect that other latent causes, working behind the scenes, and in the dark, were silently marching to the same result?

Be it remembered then, that this Indian war was but as the portico to our Revolutionary war, the fuel for which was then preparing, and which burst into a flame the ensuing year.

Neither let us forget that the Earl of Dunmore was at this time Governor of Virginia, and that he was acquainted with the views and designs of the British Cabinet, can scarcely be doubted. What then, suppose ye, would be the conduct of a man, possessing his means, filling a high official station, attached to the British Government, and master of consummate diplomatic skill?

Dunmore's penetrating eye could not but see—and he no doubt did see—two all-important objects, that if accomplished, would go to subserve and promote the grand object of the British Cabinet, viz: to establish an unbounded and unrestrained authority over our North American continent.

These two objects were, first: setting the new settlers on the west side of the Allegheny by the ears, and secondly, embroiling the Western people in a war with the Indians. These two objects accomplished, would place it in his power to direct the storm to any and every point conducive to the grand object he had in view. But as in the nature of the thing he could not; and policy forbidding that he should always appear personally in promoting and effectuating these bjects, it was necessary that he should obtain a confidential agent attached to his person and to the British government, and one that would promote his views—either publicly or covertly—as circumstances required.

The materials for his first object were abundant, and already prepared. The emigrants to the Western country were almost all from the three States of Virginia, Maryland and Pennsylvania; the line between the two States of Virginia and Pennsylvania was unsettled, and both these States claimed the whole of the Western country. This motley mixture of men from different States did not harmonize. The Virginians and Marylanders disliked the Pennsylvania laws—nor did the Pennsylvanians relish those of Virginia—thus many disputes arose, and were sometimes followed by battles, or broils, *or fisticuffs.*

The Earl of Dunmore, with becoming zeal for the honor of the Ancient Dominion, seized this state of things as propitious to his views, and having found Dr. John Conoly, of Pennsylvania, with whom, I think, he could not have had much previous acquaintance, by the art of hocus-pocus—or some other art—converted him into a staunch Virginian, and appointed him Vice-Governor and commandant at Pittsburg and dependencies; that is to say, of all the Western country. Affairs on that side of the mountain now began to wear a serious aspect. Attempts were made by both Stat s to enforce their laws, and the strong arm of power and coercion was let loose by Virginia. Some magistrates acting under the authority of Pennsylvania, were arrested, sent to Virginia, and imprisoned.

But that the reader may be well assured that the hand of Dunmore was in all this, I present him with a copy of his Proclamation. It is, however, deficient as to date.

" WHEREAS, I have reason to apprehend that the govern-"ment of Pennsylvania, in prosecution of their claims to Pitts-"burg and its dependencies, will endeavor to obstruct His "Majesty's government thereof, under my administration, by "illegal and unwarrantable commitment of the officers I have "appointed for that purpose, and that settlement is in some "danger of annoyance from the Indians also, and it being "necessary to support the dignity of His Majesty's govern-"ment, and protect his subjects in the quiet and peaceable "enjoyment of their rights. I have therefore thought proper, "by and with the consent and advice of His Majesty's coun-"cil, by this Proclamation in His Majesty's name, to order "and require the officers of the militia in that district to "embody a sufficient number of men, to repel any insult "whatsoever, and all His Majesty's liege subjects within this "colony, are hereby strictly required to be aiding and assist-"ing therein, or they shall answer the contrary at their peril; "and I further enjoin and require the several inhabitants of "the territories aforesaid, to pay His Majesty's quit-rents "and public dues to such officers as are or shall be appointed "to collect the same within this dominion, until His Majesty's "pleasure therein shall be known."

It is much to be regretted that my copy of this Proclamation is without date; there can, however, be no doubt it was issued either in 1774, or early in 1775; and I am inclined to think it was issued in 1774, but it would be satisfactory to know precisely the day, because chronology is the soul of history.

But this state of things in the West, it seems from subsequent events, was not the mere effervescence of a transient or momentary excitement, but continued a long season; the seeds of discord had fallen unhappily on ground too naturally productive, and were also too well cultivated by the Earl of Dunmore, Connoly, and the Pennsylvania officers, to evaporate in an instant.

We find by recurring to the history of our Revolutionary war, that that awful tornado, if it had not the effect to sweep away all disputes about State Rights and local interests, yet it had the effect to silence and suspend every thing of that nature pending our dubious and arduous struggle for national existence; but yet we find, in fact, that whatever conciliatory effect this state of things had upon other sections of the country, and upon the nation at large, yet it was not sufficient to extinguish this fire in the West, for in the latter end of the year 1776, or in the year 1777, we find these people petitioning Congress to interpose their authority, and redress their grievances. I have this petition before me, but it is too long to copy—I therefore only give a short abstract.

It begins with stating that whereas, Virginia and Pennsylvania both set up claims to the Western country, it was productive of the most serious and destructive consequences; that as each State pertinaciously supported their respective pretensions, the result was, as described by themselves, *"frauds, impositions, violences, depredations, animosities,"* etc.

These evils they ascribe—as indeed the fact was—to the conflicting claim of the two States; and so warm were the partisans on each side, as in some cases to produce battles and shedding of blood; but they superadd another reason for this ill humor, viz: the proceedings of Dunmore's warrant officers in laying land warrants on lands claimed by others, and many other claims for land granted by the crown of England to individuals and companies, covering a vast extent of country, and including most of the lands already settled and occupied by the greater part of the inhabitants of the western country; and they finally pray Congress to erect them into a separate State, and admit them into the Union as a fourteenth State.

As this petition recites the treaty of Pittsburg, in October, 1775, it is probable we may fix its date (for it has none) to the latter part of 1776, or 1777. I rather think the latter, not only from my own recollection of the circumstances of that period, but especially from the request in the petition to be erected into a new State, which certainly would not be thought of before the Declaration of Independence.

But the unhappy state of the western country will appear still more evident when we advert to another important document which I have also before me. It is a proclamation issued by the delegates in Congress from the States of Pennsylvania and Virginia, and bears date, " Philadelphia, July 25, 1775."

But the heat of fire, and the inflexible obstinacy of the parties engaged in this controversy, will appear in colors still stronger when we see the unavailing efforts made by the delegates in Congress from the two States of Virginia and Pennsylvania, in the year 1775. These gentlemen—it was obvious under the influence of the best of motives, and certainly with a view to the best interests, peace and happiness of the western people — sent them a proclamation, couched in terms directly calculated to restore tranquillity and harmony among them ; but the little effect produced by this proclamation their subsequent petition, just recited, and sent the next year or year after to Congress, fully demonstrates. As I consider this proclamation an important document, and nowhere recorded, I give it to the reader *verbatim, in toto:*

"*To the inhabitants of Pennsylvania and Virginia, on the west side of the Laurel Hill:*

" FRIENDS AND COUNTRYMEN: It gives us much concern "to find that disturbances have arisen, and still continue among "you, concerning the boundaries of our colonies. In the char- "acter in which we now address you, it is unnecessary to "inquire into the *origin* of those unhappy disputes, and it "would be improper for us to express our approbation or cen- "sure on either side; but as representatives of two of the colo- "nies united among many others for the defense of the liberties "of America, we think it our duty to remove, as far as lies in "our power, every obstacle that may *prevent her sons* from co- "operating as vigorously as they would wish to do toward the "attainment of this great and important end. Influenced solely "by this motive, our joint and earnest request to you is, that "all animosities which have heretofore subsisted among you, as "inhabitants of distinct colonies, may now give place to gener- "ous and concurring efforts for the preservation of everything "that can make our common country dear to us.

" We are fully persuaded that you, as well as we, wish to "see your differences terminate in this happy issue. For this "desirable purpose we recommend it to you, that all bodies of "*armed men kept up under either province* be dismissed; that all "those on either side who* *are in confinement or under bail* for "taking a part in the contest, be discharged ; and that until

---

* This word is, in the original, " we," not " who."

"the dispute be decided every person be permitted to retain "his possessions unmolested.

" By observing these directions the public tranquillity will "be secured without injury to the titles on either side; the "period, we flatter ourselves, will soon arrive when this unfor- "tunate dispute—which has produced much mischief, and, as "far as we can learn, no good—will be peaceably and constitu- "tionally determined."

" We are your friends and countrymen,

P. HENRY,
RICHARD HENRY LEE,
BENJ. HARRISON,
TH. JEFFERSON,
JOHN DICKINSON,
GEO. ROSS,
B. FRANKLIN,
JAMES WILSON,
CHA. HUMPHREYS.

" *Philadelphia, July* 25, 1775."

But to conclude this part of our subject. I think the reader cannot but see from Dunmore's proclamation the violent measures of his lieutenant, Connoly, and the Virginia officers; and from the complexion of the times, and the subsequent conduct of both Dunmore and Connoly—as we shall see hereafter—that this unhappy state of things, if not actually produced, was certainly improved by Dunmore, to subserve the views of the British Court.

We now proceed to examine the question, how far facts and circumstances justify us in supposing the Earl of Dunmore himself instrumental in producing the Indian war of 1774.

It has been already remarked that this Indian war was but the precursor to our Revolutionary war of 1775; that Dunmore, the then Governor of Virginia, was one of the most inveterate and determined enemies to the Revolution; that he was a man of high talents, especially for intrigue and diplomatic skill; that, occupying the station of Governor and Commander-in-Chief of the large and respectable State of Virginia, he possessed means and power to do much to serve the views of Great Britain.

And we have seen from the preceding pages how effectually he played his part among the inhabitants of the western country. I was present myself when a Pennsylvania magistrate, of the name of Scott, was taken into custody and brought before Dunmore, at Redstone Old Fort; he was severely threatened and dismissed, perhaps on bail, but I do not recollect now. Another Pennsylvania magistrate was sent to Staunton jail. And I have already shown in the preceding pages that there was a sufficient preparation of materials for this war in the predisposition and hostile attitude of our affairs with the Indians; that it was, consequently, no difficult matter with a Virginia Governor to direct this incipient state of things to any point most conducive to the grand end he had in view—namely, weakening our national strength in some of its best and most efficient parts. If, then, a war with the Indians might have a tendency to produce this result, it appears perfectly natural and reasonable to suppose that Dunmore would make use of all his power and influence to promote it; and, although the war of 1774 was brought to a conclusion before the year was out, yet we know that this fire was scarcely extinguished before it burst out again into a flame with tenfold fury; and two or three armies of the whites were sacrificed before we could get the Indians sub-
6

dued. And this unhappy state of our affairs with the Indians happening during the severe conflict of our Revolutionary war, had the very effect I suppose Dunmore had in view— namely, dividing our forces and enfeebling our aggregate strength; and that the seeds of these subsequent wars with the Indians were sown in 1774 and 1775, appears almost certain. Yet still, however, we admit that we are not in possession of materials to substantiate this charge against the Earl, and all we can do is to produce some facts and circumstances that deserve notice, and have a strong bearing on the case.

And the first we shall mention* is, a circular letter sent by Major Connoly, his proxy, early in the Spring of the year 1774, warning the inhabitants to be on their guard; that the Indians were very angry, and manifested so much hostility that he was apprehensive they would strike somewhere as *soon as the season would permit,* and enjoining the inhabitants to prepare and retire into forts, etc. It might be useful to collate and compare this letter with one he wrote to Captain Cresap on the 14th July following—see hereafter. In this letter he declares there is war, or danger of war, before the war is properly begun; in that to Captain Cresap he says the Indians deport themselves peaceably, when Dunmore, and Lewis, and Cornstalk are all on their march for battle.

This letter was sent by express in every direction of the country. Unhappily we have lost or mislaid it, and consequently are deficient in a most material point in its date, but from one expression in the letter, namely, he says the Indians will strike when the season permits, and this season is generally understood to mean when the leaves are out—that is, in

---

* The remark, as it should seem incidentally made in Dunmore's proclamation as to the Indian war (see page 58), deserves notice, as it has no connection with the subject of that proclamation..

the month of May. We find from a subsequent letter from Pentecost and Connoly to Captain Reece, that this assumed fact is proved—see hereafter. Therefore this letter cannot be of a later date than sometime in the month of April, and if so, before Butler's men were killed on Little Beaver, [that this was the fact, is, I think, absolutely certain, because no mention is made in Connoly's letter of this affair, which certainly would not have been omitted if precedent to this letter,] and before Logan's* family were killed on Yellow Creek, and was in fact the fiery red cross and harbinger of war, as in days of yore among the Scottish clans.

This letter produced its natural result: the people fled into forts, and put themselves into a posture of defense, and the tocsin of war resounded from Laurel Hill to the banks of the Ohio. Captain Cresap, who was peaceably at this time employed in building houses and improving lands on the Ohio, received this letter, accompanied it is believed with a confirmatory message from Colonel Croghan and Major McGee, Indian agents and interpreters, as already stated in my third

---

*Logan was the second son of Shikellemus, a celebrated chief of the Cayuga nation. This chief, on account of his attachment to the English government, was of great service to the country; having the confidence of all the Six Nations, as well as that of the English, he was very useful in settling disputes, &c., &c. He was highly esteemed by Conrad Weisser, Esq., (an officer for government in the Indian department,) with whom he acted conjunctly, and was faithful unto his death. His residence was at Shamokin, where he took great delight in acts of hospitality to such of the white people whose business led them that way. His name and fame were so high on record, that Count Zinzendorf, when in this country, in 1742, became desirous of seeing him, and actually visited him at his house in Shamokin. About the year 1772, Logan was introduced to me, by an Indian friend, as son to the late reputable chief Shikellemus, and as a friend to the white people. In the course of conversation, I thought him a man of superior talents than Indians generally were. The subject turning on vice and immorality, he confessed his too great share of this, especially his fondness for liquor. He exclaimed against the white people for imposing liquors upon the Indians; he otherwise admired their ingenuity; spoke of gentlemen, but observed the Indians unfortunately had but few of these as their neighbors, &c. He spoke of his friendship to the white people, wished always to be a neighbor to them, intended to setttle on the Ohio, below Big Beaver; was (to the best of my recollection) then encamped at the mouth of this river, (Beaver,) urged me to pay him a visit, &c. Note.—I was then living at the Moravian town on this river, in the neighborhood of Cuskuskee. In April, 1773, while on my passage down the Ohio for Muskingum, I called at Logan's settlement, where I received every civility I could expect from such of the families as were at home.—*American Pioneer, by J. S. Williams, p. 22.*

chapter,* and he thereupon immediately broke up his camp and ascended the river to Fort Wheeling, the nearest place of safety; from whence it is believed he intended speedily to return home, but during his stay at this place a report was brought into the fort that two Indians were coming down the river. Captain Cresap, supposing from every circumstance and the general aspect of affairs that war was inevitable, and in fact already begun, went up the river with his party, and two of his men, of the name of Chenoweth and Brothers, killed these two Indians; and beyond controversy this is the only circumstance in the history of this Indian war in which his name can in the remotest degree be identified with any measure tending to produce this war. And it is certain that the guilt or innocence of this affair will appear from its date. It is notorious, then, that those Indians were killed not only after Captain Cresap had received Connoly's letter, and after Butler's men were killed in the canoe, but also after the affair at Yellow Creek, and after the people had fled into forts. But more of this hereafter, when we take up Dr. Doddridge and his book—simply, however, remarking here that this affair of killing these two Indians has the same aspect and relation to Dunmore's war that the battle of Lexington had to our war of the Revolution.

But to proceed. Permit us to remark, that it is very diffi-cult at this late period to form a correct idea of those times, unless we can bring distinctly into view the real state of our frontier. The inhabitants of the western country were at this time thinly scattered from the Allegheny mountain to the eastern banks of the Ohio, and most thinly near that river. In this state of things, it was natural to suppose that the few settlers in the vicinity of Wheeling, who had collected into

---

* I had this from Captain Cresap himself a short time after it occurred.

that fort, would feel extremely solicitous to detain Captain Cresap and his men as long as possible—especially until they could see on what point the storm of war would fall. Captain Cresap, the son of a hero, and a hero himself, felt for their situation; and getting together a few more men in addition to his own, and not relishing the limits of a little fort nor a life of inactivity, set out on what was called a scouting party —that is, to reconnoitre, and scour the frontier border; and while out, and engaged in this business, fell in with and had a running fight with a party of Indians, nearly about his equal in numbers. One Indian was killed, and Cresap had one man wounded. This affair took place somewhere on the banks of the Ohio. Doddridge says it was at the mouth of Capteening; be it so—it matters not; but he adds, it was on the same day the Indians were killed in the canoe. In this the Doctor is most egregiously mistaken, as I shall prove hereafter.

But may we not ask—What were these Indians doing here at this time on the banks of the Ohio? They had no town near this place, nor was it their hunting season, as it was about the 8th or 10th of May. Is it not then probable, nay, almost certain, that this straggling banditti were prepared and ready to fall on some part of our exposed frontier, and that their dispersion saved the lives of many helpless women and children.

But the old proverb, "*Cry mad-dog, and kill him*," is, I suppose, equally as applicable to heroes as to dogs.

Captain Cresap soon after this returned to his family, in Maryland; but feeling most sensibly for the inhabitants on the frontier in their perilous situation,* immediately raised a

---

*Cresap is spoken of as remarkable for his brave, hardy, and adventurous disposition, and awarded credit for often rescuing the whites by a timely notice of the savages' approach, a knowledge of which he obtained by unceasing vigilance over their movements.—*Brantz Mayer's Address, p. 34.*

company of volunteers and marched back to their assistance, and having advanced as far as Catfish's camp—the place where Washington, Pennsylvania, now stands—he was arrested in his progress by a peremptory and insulting order from Connoly, commanding him to dismiss his men and to return home.

This order, couched in offensive and insulting language, it may be well supposed was not very grateful to a man of Captain Cresap's high sense of honor and peculiar sensibility, especially conscious as he was of the purity of his motives and the laudable end he had in view. He nevertheless obeyed, returned home and dismissed his men, and with the determination, I well know from what he said after his return, never again to take any part in the present Indian war, but to leave Mr. Commandant at Pittsburg to fight it out as he could. This hasty resolution was, however, of short duration; for however strange, contradictory and irreconcilable the conduct of the Earl of Dunmore and his Vice-Governor of Pittsburg may appear, yet it is a fact that on the 10th of June the Earl of Dunmore—unsolicited, and to Captain Cresap certainly unexpected—sent him a captain's commission of the militia of Hampshire county, Virginia, notwithstanding his residence was in Maryland. This commission reached Captain Cresap a few days after his return from the expedition to Catfish's camp, just above mentioned; and inasmuch as this commission, coming to him in the way it did, carried with it a tacit expression of the Governor's approbation of his conduct—add to which, that about the same time his feelings were daily assailed by petition after petition, from almost every section of the western country, praying, begging and beseeching him to come over to their assistance. Several of these petitions, and Dunmore's commission, have escaped the wreck of time, and are in my possession. This commission, coming at the time it did, and in the way and under the circumstances above recited, aided and strengthened as it was by the numberless petitions aforesaid, broke down and so far extinguished all Captain Cresap's personal resentment against Connoly, that he once more determined to exert all his power and influence in assisting the distressed inhabitants of the western frontier. He accordingly immediately raised a company, placed himself under the command of Major Angus McDonald, and marched with him to attack the Indians, at their town of Wappatomica, on the Muskingum. His popularity at this time was such, so many men flocked to his standard, that he could not, consistently with the rules of an army, retain them in his company, but was obliged to transfer them, much against their wills, to other captains. The result was, that after retaining in his own company as many men as he could consistently, he filled completely the company of his nephew, Captain Michael Cresap, and also partly the company of Captain Hancock Lee. This little army of about 400 men,* under Major McDonald, penetrated the Indian country as far as the Muskingum, after a smart little skirmish with a party of Indians under Captain Snake, about four miles on this side of that river, in which battle McDonald lost six men and killed the Indian chief, Captain Snake.

A little anecdote here will go to show what expert and close shooters we had in those days among our riflemen : When

---

*These men were collected from the western part of Virginia; the place of rendezvous was Wheeling, some time in the month of June, 1774. They went down the river in boats and canoes, to the mouth of Captina, from thence by the shortest route to the Wappatomica town, about sixteen miles below the present Coshocton. The pilots were Jonathan Zane, Thomas Nicholson and Tady Kelly. About six miles from the town the army was met by a party of Indians, to the number of forty or fifty, who gave a skirmish, by the way of ambuscade, in which two of our men were killed and eight or nine wounded. It was supposed that several more of them were killed, but they were carried off.—*Red Men of the Ohio Valley, by J. R. Dodge, p.* 161.

McDonald's little army arrived on the near bank of the Muskingum, and while lying there, an Indian on the opposite shore got behind a log or old tree, and was lifting up his head occasionally to view the white men's army. One of Captain Cresap's men, of the name of John Hargiss, seeing this, loaded his rifle with two balls, and placing himself on the bank of the river, watched the opportunity when the Indian raised his head, and firing at the same instant, put both balls through the Indian's neck and laid him dead,* which circumstance, no doubt, had great influence in intimidating the Indians.

McDonald, after this, had another running fight with the Indians, drove them from their towns, burnt them, destroyed their provisions, and returning to the settlement, discharged his men.

But this affair at Wappatomica and expedition of McDonald† was only the prelude to more important and efficient measures. It was well understood that the Indians were far from being subdued, and that they would now certainly collect all their force, and to the utmost of their power return the compliment of our visit to their territories.

The Governor of Virginia, whatever might have been his views as to ulterior measures, lost no time in preparing to meet this storm. He sent orders immediately to Colonel Andrew Lewis, of Augusta county, to raise an army of about

---

* The Indians dragged off the body, and buried it with the honors of war. It was found the next morning, and scalped by Hargiss. The Muskingum at this place is said to be about two hundred yards wide.

† McDonald, agreeably to Dunmore's orders, after a dreary march through the wilderness, had rendezvoused his four hundred men at Wheeling creek in June, and, from this place, it was resolved to invade the Indian territory on the head waters of the Muskingum, and to destroy the Wappatomica towns. The results of this expedition were not of remarkable value in the campaign, though the Indian towns were destroyed by the invaders after the savages had fled. McDonald and his men were harassed by the foe, and being short of provisions, returned with dispatch to Wheeling.—*Discourse by Brantz Mayer, delivered before the Maryland Historical Society, p.* 58.

one thousand men, and to march with all expedition to the mouth of the Great Kanawha, on the Ohio river, where, or at some other point, he would join him after he had got together another army, which he intended to raise in the northwestern counties and command in person. Lewis lost no time, but collected the number of men required, and marched without delay to the appointed place of rendezvous.

But the Earl was not quite so rapid in his movements, which circumstance the eagle eye of old Cornstalk, the general of the Indian army, saw, and was determined to avail himself of, foreseeing that it would be much easier to destroy two separate columns of an invading army before than after their junction and consolidation. With this view, he marched with all expedition to attack Lewis before he was joined by the Earl's army from the north—calculating confidently, no doubt, that if he could destroy Lewis he would be able to give a good account of the army under the Earl.

The plans of Cornstalk appear to have been those of a consummate and skillful general, and the prompt and rapid execution of them displayed the energy of a warrior. He therefore, without loss of time, attacked Lewis at his post. The attack was sudden, violent, and I believe unexpected; it was nevertheless well fought, very obstinate, and of long continuance, and as both parties fought with rifles, the conflict was dreadful; many were killed on both sides, and the contest was only finished with the approach of night. The Virginians, however, kept the field, but lost many valuable officers and men, and among the rest Colonel Charles Lewis, brother to the Commander-in-Chief.

Cornstalk and Blue Jacket, the two Indian captains, it is said performed prodigies of valor; but finding at length all their efforts unavailing, drew off their men in good order, and with the determination to fight no more if peace could be obtained upon reasonable terms.

This battle of Lewis's opened an easy and unmolested passage for Dunmore through the Indian country;* but it is proper to remark here, however, that when Dunmore arrived with his wing of the army at the mouth of the Hocking, he sent Captain White-eyes, a Delaware chief, to invite the Indians to a treaty, and he remained stationary at that place until White-eyes returned, who reported that the Indians would not treat about peace. I presume, in order of time this must have been just before Lewis's battle, because it will appear in the sequel of this story that a great revolution took place in the minds of the Indians after the battle.

Dunmore, immediately upon the report of White-eyes that the Indians were not disposed for peace, sent an express to Colonel Lewis to move on and meet him near Chillicothe, on the Scioto, and both wings of the army were put in motion. But as Dunmore† approached the Indian towns he was met by flags from the Indians demanding peace, to which he acceded, halted his army, and runners were sent to invite the Indian chiefs, who cheerfully obeyed the summons and came to the treaty, save only Logan, the great orator, who refused to come. It seems, however, that neither Dunmore nor the Indian chiefs considered his presence of much importance, for

---

* A little anecdote will prove that Dunmore was a general, and also the high estimation in which he held Captain Cresap. While the army was marching through the Indian country Dunmore ordered Captain Cresap with his company and some more of his best troops in the rear. This displeased Cresap, and he expostulated with the Earl, who replied, that the reason of this arrangement was, because he knew that if he was attacked in front all those men would soon rush forward into the engagement. This reason—which was, by the by, a handsome compliment—satisfied Cresap and all the rear guard.

† John Gibson, in the year 1774, accompanied Lord Dunmore on the expedition against the Shawanese and other Indians on the Scioto; that on their arrival within *fifteen miles* of the towns they were met by a flag and a *white man* by the name of Elliot, who informed Lord Dunmore that the chiefs of the Shawanese had sent to request his lordship *to halt his army and send in* some person who understood their language; that this deponent, *at the request of Lord*

they went to work and finished the treaty without him—referring, I believe, some unsettled points for future discussion at a treaty to be held the ensuing Summer or Fall, at Pittsburg. This treaty—the articles of which I never saw, nor do I know that they were ever recorded—concluded Dunmore's war, in September or October, 1774. After the treaty was over, old Cornstalk, the Shawanee chief, accompanied Dunmore's army until they reached the mouth of Hocking, on the Ohio ; and what was most singular, he rather made his home in Captain Cresap's tent, with whom he continued on terms of the most friendly familiarity. I consider this circumstance as positive proof that the Indians themselves neither considered Captain Cresap the murderer of Logan's family nor the cause of the war. It appears, also, that at this place the Earl of Dunmore received dispatches from England. Doddridge says he received these on his march out.

But we ought to have mentioned in its proper place, that after the treaty between Dunmore and the Indians commenced near Chillicothe, Lewis arrived with his army and encamped two or three miles from Dunmore, which so alarmed the Indians, as they thought he was so much irritated at losing so many men in the late battle that he would not easily be pacified ; nor would they be satisfied until Dunmore and old Cornstalk went into Lewis's camp to converse with him.

Dr. Doddridge represents this affair in different shades of

Dunmore, and the whole of the officers with him, went in; that on his arrival at the towns, Logan, the Indian, came to where this deponent was sitting with the Cornstalk, and the other chiefs of the Shawanese, and asked him to walk out with him; that they went in to a copse of wood when they sat down, when Logan, after shedding abundance of tears, delivered to him the speech, *nearly* as related by Mr. Jefferson in his Notes on the State of Virginia; that he the deponent, *told him then that it was not Colonel* CRESAP *who had murdered his relatives,* and although *his son,* Captain Michael Cresap, was *with* the party who had killed a *Shawanese* chief and *other* Indians, yet he was *not* present when HIS RELATIVES were killed at Baker's, near the mouth of Yellow Creek, on the Ohio; that this deponent, *on his return to camp,* delivered the speech to Lord Dunmore; and that the murders perpetrated as above *were considered* as ultimately the cause of the war of 1774, commonly called CRESAP'S WAR.—*Appendix to Brantz Mayer's Address before the Maryland Historical Society,* p. 76.

light from this statement. I can only say, I have my information from an officer who was present at the time.

But it is time to remind the reader that, although I have wandered into such a minute detail of the various occurrences, facts and circumstances of Dunmore's war—and all of which as a history may be interesting to the present and especially to the rising generation—yet it is proper to remark that I have two leading objects chiefly in view: First, to convince the world that, whoever and whatever might be the cause of the Indian war of 1774, it was not Captain Cresap; secondly, that from the aspect of our political affairs at that period, and from the known hostility of Dunmore to the American Revolution, and withal from the subsequent conduct of Dunmore, and the dreadful Indian war that commenced soon after the beginning of our war with Great Britain—I say, from all these circumstances we have infinitely stronger reason to suspect Dunmore than Cresap; and I may say that the dispatches above mentioned, that were received by Dunmore at Hocking, although after the treaty, yet were calculated to create suspicion.*

But if, as we suppose, that Dunmore was secretly at the bottom of this Indian war, it is evident that he could not with propriety appear personally in a business of this kind; and we have seen, and shall see, how effectually his sub-gov-

---

* In Burk's History of Virginia, vol. 4, p. 74, the reader will find a further development of Connoly's subsequent conduct and hostility to American interests, as disclosed in the plot formed by Lord Dunmore to bring the Indian tribes of the West into the Revolutionary conflict. He had been commissioned by the Earl as a Lieutenant Colonel Commandant. [4th Burk, Appendix 4.] The joint plans of these loyal Britons show the great probability that there was, in truth, a scheme in embryo to crush the American Revolution at its birth, by a union between the Indians, negroes and loyalists, and by the excitement of an Indian war on the frontier, which would compel the settlers to think of self-protection against savages, instead of demanding from England the security of rights and liberty, at the point of the sword or muzzle of the rifle. By a letter from Lord Dartmouth to Lord Dunmore, dated at Whitehall on the 2d August, 1775, it appears that, *in the previous May*, Dunmore had communicated to the home government his vile plan of raising the Indians and negroes to join the miscalled loyalists in an onslaught against the Americans.—*Brantz Mayer's Address, p.* 41.

ernor played his part between the Virginians and Pennsylvanians, and it now remains for us to examine how far the conduct of this man (Connoly) will bear us out in the supposition that there was also some foul play, some dark, intriguing work to embroil the western country in an Indian war.

And I think it best, now, as we have introduced this man Connoly again, to give the reader a short, condensed history of his whole proceedings, that we may have him in full view at once. We have already presented the reader with his circular letter, and its natural results and consequences, and also with his insulting letter and mandatory order to Captain Cresap at Catfish's camp, to dismiss his men and go home; and that the reader may now see a little of the character of this man, and understand him—if it is possible to understand him—I present him with the copy of a letter to Captain Reece:

"As I have received intelligence that Logan,* a Mingo "Indian, with about twenty Shawanese and others, were to "set off for war last Monday, and I have reason to believe "that they may come upon the inhabitants about Wheeling,

---

* One of the incidents attending this incursion deserves to be mentioned, as illustrating the character of Logan. While hovering, with his followers, around the skirts of a thick settlement, he suddenly came within view of a small field, recently cleared, in which three men were pulling flax. Causing the greater part of his men to remain where they were, Logan, together with two others, crept up within long shot of the white men and fired. One man fell dead, the remaining two attempted to escape. The elder of the fugitives (Hellew,) was quickly overtaken and made prisoner by Logan's associates, while Logan himself, having thrown down his rifle, pressed forward alone in pursuit of the younger of the white men, whose name was Robinson. The contest was keen for several hundred yards, but Robinson, unluckily, looking around, in order to have a view of his pursuer, ran against a tree with such violence as completely to stun him, and render him insensible for several minutes.

Upon recovering, he found himself bound and lying upon his back, while Logan sat by his side, with unmoved gravity, awaiting his recovery. He was then compelled to accompany them in their further attempts upon the settlements, and in the course of a few days, was marched off with great rapidity for their villages in Ohio. During the march, Logan remained silent and melancholy, probably brooding over the total destruction of his family. The prisoners, however, were treated kindly, until they arrived at an Indian village upon the

7

"I hereby order, require and command you, with all the "men you can raise, immediately to march and join *any of* "*the companies already out and under the pay of the Govern-* "*ment*, and, upon joining your parties together, scour the "frontier and become a barrier to our settlements, and en- "deavor to fall in with their tracks and pursue them, using "your utmost endeavors to chastise them as open and avowed "enemies.

"I am, sir, your most humble servant,

"Dorsey Pentecost, for

"JOHN CONNOLY.

"*Captain Joel Reece:*   Use all expedition.   May 27, 1774."

Now, here is a fellow for you.   A very short time before this, perhaps two or three days before the date of this letter, Captain Cresap, who had a fine company of volunteers, was insulted, ordered to dismiss his men and go home ; and indeed it appears from one expression in this letter—namely, "*the companies who are already out*"—that these companies must have been actually out at the very time Cresap was ordered home.

Muskingum.   When within a mile of the town, Logan became more animated, and uttered the "scalp hallo" several times, in the most terrrible tones.   The never failing scene of insult and torture then began.   Crowds flocked out to meet them, and a line was formed for the gauntlet.

Logan took no share in the cruel game, but did not attempt to repress it.   He, however, gave Robinson, whom he regarded as his own prisoner, some directions as to the best means of reaching the council house in safety, and displayed some anxiety for his safe arrival, while poor Hellew was left in total ignorance, and permitted to struggle forward as he best could. Robinson, under the patronage of Logan, escaped with a few slight bruises, but Hellew, not knowing where to run, was dreadfully mangled, and would probably have been killed upon the spot, had not Robinson (not without great risk on his own part) seized him by the hand and dragged him into the council house.

On the following morning, a council was called in order to determine their fate, in which Logan held a conspicuous superiority over all who were assembled.   Hellew's destiny came first under discussion, and was quickly decided by an almost unanimous vote of adoption. Robinson's was most difficult to determine.   A majority of the council (partly influenced by a natural thirst for vengeance upon at least *one* object, partly, perhaps, by a lurking jealousy of the most imposing superiority of Logan's character,) were obstinately bent upon putting him to death.   Logan spoke for nearly an hour upon the question ; and if Robinson is to be

Now, if any man is skilled in the art of legerdemain, let him unriddle this enigma if he can.

But, as so many important facts crowd together at this eventful period, it may be satisfactory to the reader, and have a tendency more clearly to illustrate the various scenes interwoven in the thread of this history, to present to his view a chronological list of these facts ; and I think the first that deserves notice is Connoly's circular letter, which we date the 25th day of April; secondly, the two men killed in Butler's canoe we know was the 1st or 2d day of May ; thirdly, the affair at Yellow Creek was on the 3d or 4th day of May ; fourthly, the Indians killed in the canoe above Wheeling the 5th or 6th day of May; fifthly, the skirmish with the Indians on the river Ohio about the 8th or 10th day of May; after which Captain Cresap, returning home, raised a company of volunteers and returned to Catfish's camp about the 25th of May. Indeed, this fact speaks for itself; it could not be earlier, when it is considered that he rode home from the Ohio, a distance of about 140 miles, raised a company and marched back as far as Catfish, through bad roads, near 120

---

believed, with an energy, copiousness, and dignity, which would not have disgraced Henry himself. He appeared at no loss for either words or ideas; his tones were deep and musical, and were heard by the assembly with the silence of death. All, however, was vain. Robinson was condemned, and within an hour afterward, was fastened to the stake. Logan stood apart from the crowd with his arms folded, and his eyes fixed upon the scene with an air of stern displeasure.

When the fire was about to be applied, he suddenly strode into the circle, pushing aside those who stood in the way, and advancing straight up to the stake, cut the cords with his tomahawk, and taking the prisoner by the hand, led him with a determined air to his own wigwam. The action was so totally unexpected, and the air of the chief so determined, that he had reached the door of his wigwam before any one ventured to interfere. Much dissatisfaction was then expressed, and threatening symptoms of a tumult appeared; but so deeply rooted was his authority, that in a few hours all was quiet, and Robinson, without opposition, was permitted to enter an Indian family. He remained with Logan until the treaty of Fort Pitt, in the autumn of the ensuing year, when he returned to Virginia. He ever retained the most unbounded admiration for Logan, and repeatedly declared that his countenance, when speaking, was the most striking, varied, and impressive, that he ever beheld. And when it is recollected that he had often heard Lee and Henry, in all their glory, the compliment must be regarded as a very high one.—*Appendix to Western Adventure, by John A. McClung, p.* 278.

miles—and all, agreeable to my statement, in seventeen days. Then it is evident he was not at Catfish's camp sooner than the 25th of May; and if so, he was ordered home at the very time when scouts were out, and the settlement threatened with an attack from the Indians, as is manifest from Connoly's own letter to Captain Reece, dated May 27, 1774.

But the hostility of Connoly to Captain Cresap was unremitting, and without measure or decency; for on the 14th of July, of the same year, we find one of the most extraordinary, crooked, malignant, Grubstreet epistles that ever appeared upon paper. But let us see it:

"FORT DUNMORE, July 14, 1774.

"Your whole proceedings, so far as relate to our disturb-
"ances with the Indians, have been of a nature so extraord-
"inary, that I am much at a loss to account for the cause;
"but when I consider your late steps, tending directly to
"ruin the service here, by inveigling away the militia of this
"garrison by your preposterous proposals, and causing them
"thereby to embezzle the arms of Government, purchased at
"an enormous expense, and at the same time to reflect infinite
"disgrace upon the honor of this colony by attacking a set of
"people which, notwithstanding the injury they have sus-
"tained by you in the loss of their people, yet continue to
"rely upon the professions of friendship which I have made,
"and deport themselves accordingly—I say, when I consider
"these matters I must conclude that you are actuated by a
"spirit of discord so prejudicial to the peace and good order
"of society, that the conduct calls for justice, and due execu-
"tion thereof can only check. I must once again order you
"to desist from your pernicious designs, and require of you, if
"you are an officer of militia, to send the deserters from this

"place back with all expedition, that they may be dealt with
"as their crimes merit.

"I am, sir, your servant,

"JOHN CONNOLY."

This letter, although short, contains so many things for
remark and animadversion, that we scarcely know where to
begin. It exhibits, however, a real picture of the man, and
a mere superficial glance at its phraseology will prove that he
is angry, and his nerves in a tremor. It is, in fact, an inco-
herent jumble of words and sentences, all in the disjunctive.
But it is a perfect original and anomaly in the epistolary line,
and contains in itself internal marks of genuine authenticity.

The first thing in this letter that calls for our attention, is
the language he uses toward the people he calls "*militia
deserters.*" "That they may be dealt with," he says, "as
their crimes merit." Now, I pray you, who were those
people? Doubtless the respectable farmers and others in
the vicinity of Pittsburg. And what does this Mogul of the
West intend to do with them? Why, hang them, to be
sure, for this is military law. But the true state of this case
doubtless is, that these militia considered themselves free
men; that they were not well pleased either with Connoly or
garrison duty; that, viewing their country in danger, and
their wives and children exposed to savage barbarity, preferred more active service, and joined the standard of Captain
Cresap. And is this a new thing, or reprehensible? How
often do our militia enter into the regular army, and who
ever dreamed of hanging them for so doing?

But secondly, we say, it is possible Captain Cresap did not
know from whence these men came; and if he did, he deserves
no censure for receiving them. And as to the charge of in-

veigling away the militia from the garrison, we know this must be positively false, because he was not in Pittsburg in the year 1774, either personally or by proxy.

As to the general charge against Captain Cresap of attacking the Indians, and the great injury he had done them, I need only say, this charge is refuted again and again in the course of this history; and its unparalleled impudence, especially at the date of this letter, merits the deepest contempt. But the most extraordinary feature in this most extraordinary letter is couched in these words, namely : *" That the Indians relied upon the expressions of friendship he made them, and deported themselves accordingly."*

Be astonished, oh ye nations of the earth, and all ye kindreds of the people, at this ! For be it remembered that this is the 14th day of July, 1774, when Connoly has the unblushing impudence to assert that the Indians relied upon his expressions of friendship and deported themselves accordingly, when at this very time we were engaged in the hottest part of Dunmore's war; when ·Dunmore himself was raising an army, and personally on his way to take the command ; when Lewis was on his march from Augusta county, Virginia, to the Ohio; and when Cornstalk,* with his Indian army, was in motion to meet Lewis; and when Captain Cresap was

---

* Cornstalk and Elenipsico, his son, were killed during a friendly visit to Point Pleasant, in the summer of 1775, only a few months after the action. The circumstances attending the affair are thus related by Colonel Stewart :

" A Captain Arbuckle commanded the garrison of the fort erected at Point Pleasant after the battle fought by General Lewis with the Indians at that place, in October, 1774. In the succeeding year, when the Revolutionary war had commenced, the agents of Great Britain exerted themselves to excite the Indians to hostility against the United States. The mass of the Shawnees entertained a strong animosity against the Americans. But, two of their chiefs, Cornstalk and Red Hawk, not participating in that animosity, visited the garrison at the Point, where Arbuckle continued to command. Colonel Stewart was at the post in the character of a volunteer, and was an eye-witness of the facts which he relates. Cornstalk represented his unwillingness to take a part in the war, on the British side; but stated, that his nation, except himself and his tribe, were determined on war with us, and he supposed that he and his people would be compelled to go with the stream.

"On this intimation, Arbuckle resolved to detain the two chiefs, and a third Shawnee who

actually raising a company to join Dunmore when he arrived. And it was while engaged in this business that he received this letter from Connoly.

Now, if any man can account for this strange and extraordinary letter upon rational principles, let him do so if he can ; he has more ingenuity and a more acute discernment than I have.

Soon after receiving this letter, Captain Cresap left his company on the west side of the mountain and rode home, where he met the Earl of Dunmore at his own house, and where he (the Earl) remained a few days in habits of friendship and cordiality with the family. One day, while the Earl was at his house, Captain Cresap, finding him alone, introduced the subject of Connoly's ill treatment—with a view, I suppose, of obtaining redress, or of exposing the character of a man he knew high in the estimation and confidence of the Earl. But what effect, suppose ye, had this remonstrance on the Earl ? I'll tell you : it lulled him into a profound sleep ! Aye, aye—thinks I to myself, young as I then was—this will not do, Captain ; there are wheels within wheels, dark things behind the curtain, between this noble Earl and his subsatellite.

Captain Cresap was himself open, candid and unsuspicious,

---

came with them to the fort, as hostages, under the expectation of preventing thereby any hostile efforts of the nation. On the day before these unfortunate Indians fell victims to the fury of the garrison, Elenipsico, the son of Cornstalk, repaired to Point Pleasant for the purpose of visiting his father, and on the next day, two men belonging to the garrison, whose names were Hamilton and Gillmore, crossed the Kanawha, intending to hunt in the woods beyond it. On their return from hunting, some Indians who had come to view the position at the Point, concealed themselves in the weeds near the mouth of the Kanawha, and killed Gillmore while endeavoring to pass them. Colonel Stewart and Captain Arbuckle were standing on the opposite bank of the river at that time, and were surprised that a gun had been fired so near the fort, in violation of orders which had been issued inhibiting such an act.

"Hamilton ran down the bank, and cried out that Gillmore was killed. Captain Hall commanded the company to which Gillmore belonged. His men leaped into a canoe, and hastened to the relief of Hamilton. They brought the body of Gillmore weltering in blood, and the head scalped, across the river. The canoe had scarcely reached the shore, when Hall's men cried out, 'let us kill the Indians in the fort.' Captain Hall placed himself in front of his

and I do not know what he thought; but I well remember my own thoughts upon this occasion.

But that we may, as nearly as possible, finish our business with Connoly, although we must thereby get a little ahead of our history; yet, as already remarked, we think it less perplexing to the reader than to give him here a little and there a little of this extraordinary character.

We find, then, that in the year 1775, Connoly, finding that his sheepskin could not cover him much longer, threw off the mask and fled to his friend Dunmore, who also, about the same time, was obliged to take sanctuary on board a British ship-of-war in the Chesapeake Bay; from this place—*i. e.*, Portsmouth, in Virginia—Connoly wrote the following letter to Colonel John Gibson, who, no doubt, he supposed possessed sentiments somewhat congenial with his own. It happened, however, that he was mistaken in his man, for Gibson exposed him, and put his letter into the hands of the commissioners who were holding a treaty with the Indians. But let us see this letter. It is dated—

"PORTSMOUTH, August 9, 1775.

"*Dear Sir:* I have safely arrived here, and am happy in "the greatest degree at having so fortunately escaped the

---

soldiers, and they ascended the river's bank, pale with rage, and carrying their loaded firelocks in their hands. Colonel Stewart and Captain Arbuckle exerted themselves in vain to dissuade these men, exasperated to madness by the spectacle of Gillmore's corpse, from the cruel deed which they contemplated. They cocked their guns, threatening those gentlemen with instant death if they did not desist, and rushed into the fort.

"The interpreter's wife, who had been a captive among the Indians and felt an affection for them, ran to their cabin and informed them that Hall's soldiers were advancing, with the intention of taking their lives, because they believed that the Indians who killed Gillmore had come with Cornstalk's son on the preceding day. This the young man solemnly denied, and averred that he knew nothing of them. His father, perceiving that Elenipsico was in great agitation, encouraged him and advised him not to fear. 'If the Great Spirit,' said he, 'has sent you here to be killed, you ought to die like a man!' As the soldiers approached the door, Cornstalk rose to meet them, and received seven or eight balls, which instantly terminated his existence. His son was shot dead in the seat which he occupied. The Red Hawk made an attempt to climb the chimney, but fell by the fire of some of Hall's men."—*Appendix to Western Adventure, by John A. McClung, p. 286.*

"narrow inspection of my enemies—the enemies to their "country's good order and government. I should esteem "myself defective in point of friendship toward you, should I "neglect to caution you to avoid an over-zealous exertion of "what is now ridiculously called 'patriotic spirit;' but on "the contrary, to deport yourself with that moderation for "which you have always been so remarkable, and which "must in this instance tend to your honor and advantage. "You may rest assured from me, sir, that the greatest una- "nimity now prevails at home, and the innovating spirit "among us here is looked upon as ungenerous and undutiful; "and that the utmost exertions of the powers in Government "(if necessary) will be used to convince the infatuated people "of their folly.

"I would, I assure you, sir, give you such convincing proofs "of what I assert, and from which every reasonable person "may conclude the effects, that nothing but madness could "operate upon a man so far as to overlook his duty to the "present Constitution, and to form unwarrantable associations "with *enthusiasts*, whose ill-timed folly must draw down upon "them inevitable destruction. His Lordship desires you to "present his hand to Captain White-eyes,* and to assure him "he is sorry he had not the pleasure of seeing him at the "treaty, [a treaty held by Connoly in his name,] or that the "situation of affairs prevented him from coming down.

"Believe me, dear sir, that I have no motive in writing "sentiments thus to you, further than to endeavor to steer you "clear of the misfortunes which I am confident must involve "but unhappily too many. I have sent you an address from "the people of Great Britain to the people of America, and "desire you to consider it attentively, which will, I flatter

---

* A Delaware Indian Chief.

"myself, convince you of the idleness of many determinations, "and the absurdity of an intended slavery.

"Give my love to George, [his brother, afterward a Colonel "in the Revolutionary war,] and tell him he shall hear from "me, and I hope to his advantage. Interpret the inclosed "speech to Captain White-eyes, from his Lordship. Be pre- "vailed upon to shun the popular error, and judge for your- "self, as a good subject, and expect the rewards due to your "services. I am, &c.,

"JOHN CONNOLY."

The inclosed speech to White-eyes we shall see in its proper place, after we have finished our business with Connoly. It seems, then, that either a mistaken notion of his own influence, or greatly deceived by his calculations on the support of Colonel Gibson, his brother and friends, or in obedience to the solicitations of his friend Dunmore, he undertakes, *incog.*, a hazardous journey from the Chesapeake Bay to Pittsburg, in company, if I recollect right, with a certain Dr. Smith; but our Dutch republicans of Fredericktown, Maryland, smelt a rat, seized and imprisoned him* in limbo, from whence he was removed to the Philadelphia jail, where we will leave him awhile to cool. But let us now look at these two characters. Connoly uses every effort to destroy us and subvert our liberties, and Cresap marches to Boston with a company of riflemen to defend his country. If, then, men's actions afford us the true and best criterion to judge of

---

* The original papers relative to the arrest of Connoly and his incendiary companions in Maryland in 1775 are recorded in the MS. "Journal of the Committee of Observation of the Middle District of Frederick County," under date of 21 Nov., 1775, in the possession of the Maryland Historical Society. This record gives 1st: the letter from John Connoly to John Gibson, dated at Portsmouth, Aug. 9, 1775; 2d: A letter from Lord Dunmore to the Indian Captain White-eyes. It contains a *loving* message to "*his brother*" The Cornstalk—(the same who had fought at Point Pleasant); 3d: Proposals to General Gage for raising an army to the Westward for the purpose of effectually obstructing a communication between the Southern and Northern Governments. One of the chief proposals was to raise the Indians.— *Brantz Mayer's Address, p.* 41.

their merit or demerit, we can be at no loss to decide on this occasion.

Nor can there be any doubt that this man, so full of tender sensibility and sympathy for the sufferings of the Indians, when arrested with his colleague, Smith, in Frederick, had a Pandora's box full of firebrands, arrows and death, to scatter among the inhabitants of the West.

But it is probable the reader, as well as the writer, is weary of such company. We therefore bid him adieu, and once more attend His Excellency the Governor of Virginia, whom we left, I think, on board a British sloop-of-war in the Chesapeake Bay, and to avoid confusion in our narrative took up Connoly, and have been so long paying our respects to him as almost to have forgotten the Earl.

The reader has not forgotten, we presume, that we long since stated it as our opinion that it was probable, and that we had strong reasons to believe, that Dunmore himself, from political motives, though acting behind the scenes, was in reality at the bottom of the Indian war of 1774. We have already alluded to several circumstances previous to and during that war, but we have in reserve several more, evincing the same fact, subsequent to the war.

It may be remembered that at the treaty of Chillicothe it was remarked that some points were referred for future discussion at Pittsburg, in the ensuing Fall; and it appears that a treaty was actually held by Connoly, in Dunmore's name, with the chiefs of the Delaware and some Mingo tribes in the Summer ensuing. And this is historically a fact, and matter of record, which I extract from the minutes of a treaty* held in the Autumn of the same year with several

---

* The original minutes of this treaty are in my possession. It was presented to me by my friend John Madison, Secretary to the Commissioners.

tribes of Indians, by commissioners from the Congress of the United States and from Virginia.

But to understand this perfectly, the reader must be informed that previous to this treaty Captain James Wood,* afterward Governor of Virginia, was sent by that State as the herald of peace, with the olive branch in his hand, to invite all the Indian tribes bordering on the Ohio and its waters, to a treaty at Pittsburg, on the 10th day of September following. Captain Wood kept a journal, which is incorporated in the proceedings of the treaty, from which journal I copy, as follows:

"July the 9th, I arrived at Fort Pitt, where I received "information that the chiefs of the Delawares and a few of "the Mingoes had lately been treating with Major Connoly, "agreeable to instruction from Lord Dunmore, and that the "Shawanese had not come to the treaty," &c.

Captain Wood, however, acknowledges in a letter he wrote to the Convention of Virginia from this place, that this treaty held by Connoly was *in the most open and candid manner; that it was held in the presence of the committee, and that he laid the Governor's instructions before them.* Very good. But why these remarks respecting Connoly and Dunmore? Does not this language imply jealousy and suspicion, which Captain Wood—who certainly was deceived—was anxious to remove? But to proceed. He says:

---

* On the 25th of July, 1775, Captain James Wood having been sent with a single companion to invite the Western Indians to a treaty at Fort Pitt, encountered Logan and several other Mingoes who had been prisoners at that post. He found them *all deeply intoxicated* and inquisitive as to their designs. To his appeal the savages made no definite reply, but represented the tribes as very angry. The wayfarers bivouacked near the Indian town, and about ten o'clock at night one of the savages stole into the camp and stamped upon the sleeper's head. Starting to his feet and arousing his companion, Wood and the interpreter found several Indians around them armed with knives and tomahawks. For awhile the Americans seemed to have pacified the red men, but as a friendly squaw apprized them that the savages meditated their death, they stole away for concealment in the recesses of the forest. When they returned

"*July* 10.—White-eyes came, with an interpreter, to my
"lodging. He informed me he was desirous of going to Wil-
"liamsburg with Mr. Connoly, to see Lord Dunmore, who
"had promised him his interest in procuring a grant from
"the King for the lands claimed by the Delawares ; that they
"were all desirous of living as the white people do, and under
"their laws and protection ; that Lord Dunmore had engaged
"to make him some satisfaction for his trouble in going sev-
"eral times to the Shawanee towns, and serving with him on
"the campaign, &c. He told me he hoped I would advise
"him whether it was proper for him to go or not. I was
"then under the necessity of acquainting him with the dis-
"putes subsisting between Lord Dunmore and the people of
"Virginia, and engaged whenever the assembly met that I
"would go with him to Williamsburg, &c. He was very
"thankful, and appeared satisfied."

The reader must observe this is July the 10th, 1775; and
if he will please to refer to page 75, he will see from Con-
noloy's letter of August 9th how much reliance was to be
placed on his candor and sincerity, as stated by Captain
Wood to the Convention on the 9th day of July. Thus we
find that about thirty days after Captain Wood's testimony
in his favor, Connoly threw away the mask and presented
himself in his true character; and from his own confession,
and the tenor of his letter to Gibson, it is plain that the
current of suspicion ran so strongly against him that he de-

again to the Indian town after daylight, Logan repeated the foul story of the murder of his
"mother, sister, and all his relations" by the people of Virginia. By turns he wept and sang.
Then he dwelt and gloated over the revenge he had taken for his wrongs; and finally, he told
Wood that several of his fellows, who had long been prisoners at Fort Pitt, desired to kill the
American messengers, and demanded if the forester was afraid ? " No ! " replied Wood, " we
are bùt two lone men, sent to deliver the message we have given to the tribes. We are in
your power ; we have no means of defence, and you may kill us if you think proper ! "
" Then," exclaimed Logan, apparently confounded by their coolness and courage, " you shall
not be hurt ! "—nor were they, for the ambassadors departed unmolested to visit the Wyandotte
towns.—*Discourse by Brantz Mayer, p.* 65.

8

clared himself "*most happy in escaping the vigilance of his enemies.*"

We owe the reader an apology for introducing this man again; but the fact is, that Dunmore and Connoly are so identified in all the political movements of this period that we can seldom see one without the other; and Connoly is the more prominent character, especially in the affairs of the West.

But we now proceed with Captain Wood's journal. He tells us that, on the 20th of July, he met Garrett Pendergrass about 9 o'clock; that he had just left the Delaware towns; that two days before the Delawares had just returned from the Wyandots' towns, where they had been at a grand council with a French and English officer and the Wyandots; that Monsieur Baubee and the English officer told them to be on their guard, that the white people intended to strike them very soon, &c.

"*July* 21.—At 1 o'clock, arriving at the Moravian Indian "town, examined the minister (a Dutchman), concerning the "council lately held with the Indians, &c., who confirmed the "account before stated.

"*July* 22.—About 10 o'clock arrived at Coshocton (a chief "town of the Delawares), and delivered to their council a "speech, which they answered on the 23d. After expressing "their thankfulness for the speech, and willingness to attend "the proposed treaty at Pittsburg, they delivered to Captain "Wood a belt and string that they said were sent to them by "an Englishman and Frenchman from Detroit, accompanied "with a message that the people of Virginia were determined to "strike them; that they would come upon them two different "ways—the one by the way of the lakes, and the other by "way of the Ohio, and the Virginians were determined to

"drive them off and to take their lands ; that they must be
"constantly on their guard, and not to give any credit to
"whatever you said, as you were a people not to be depended
"upon; that the Virginians would invite them to a treaty, but
"that they must not go at any rate, and to take particular
"notice of the advice they gave, which proceeded from mo-
"tives of real friendship."

Now, by comparing and collating this with the speech sent
from Dunmore, inclosed in Connoly's letter, it will furnish us
with a squinting at the game that was playing with the Indians by the Earl of Dunmore and other British officers—to
be convinced of which, read the following speech from Dunmore : *

"*Brother Captain White-eyes:* I am glad to hear your good
"speeches, as sent to me by Major Connoly; and you may
"be assured I shall put one end of the belt you have sent
"me into the hands of our great King, who will be glad to
"hear from his brothers, the Delawares, and will take strong
"hold of it. You may rest satisfied that our foolish young
"men shall never be permitted to have your lands, but on
"the contrary the great King will protect you, and preserve
"you in the possession of them.

"Our young people in this country have been very foolish,
"and have done many imprudent things, for which they must
"soon be sorry, and of which I make no doubt they have
"acquainted you; but I must desire you not to listen to them,
"as they would be willing you should act foolishly with them-
"selves ; but rather let what you hear pass in at one ear and
"out of the other, so that it may make no impression on your
"heart, *until you hear from me fully*, which shall be as soon
"as I can give further information.

---

* This speech was inclosed in a letter to Gibson.

"Captain White-eyes will please acquaint the Cornstalk*
"with these my sentiments, as well as the chiefs of the Min-
"goes and other Six Nations.

[Signed]　　　　　　　　　　　　　　　"DUNMORE."

It is scarcely necessary to remark here that the flight of
Dunmore from Williamsburg, of Connoly from Pittsburg,
this speech of Dunmore's, and the speech of the Delawares
to Captain Wood, are all nearly cotemporaneous, and point
the reader pretty clearly to the aspect of our affairs with the
Indians at this period. Dunmore's speech, as you have it
above, although pretty explicit, is yet guarded, as it had to
pass through an equivocal medium; but he tells Captain
White-eyes he shall hear from him *hereafter;* and this *hereafter* speech was no doubt in Connoly's portmanteau when he
was arrested in Frederick.

But to conclude this tedious chapter. Nothing more now
seems necessary than to call the attention of the reader to
those inferences that the facts and circumstances detailed in
the foregoing pages seem to warrant. The first circumstance
in the order of events seems to be the extraordinary and contradictory conduct of Dunmore and Connoly respecting Captain Cresap. They certainly understood each other, and had
one ultimate end in view; yet we find on all occasions Dunmore treats Cresap with the utmost confidence and cordiality,

---

* Few, if any, chiefs in history are spoken of in terms of higher commendation than
Cornstalk, sachem of the Shawanese, and king of the Northern Confederacy in 1774, a chief
remarkable for many great and good qualities. He was disposed to be at all times the friend
of white men, as he ever was the advocate of honorable peace. But when his country's
wrongs "called aloud for battle, " he became the thunderbolt of war, and made her oppressors
feel the weight of his uplifted arm. His noble bearing, his generous and disinterested attachment to the colonies when the thunder of British cannon was reverberating through the land,
his anxiety to preserve the frontier of Virginia from desolation and death (the object of his
visit to Point Pleasant), all conspired to win for him the esteem and respect of others; while
the untimely and perfidious manner of his death caused a deep and lasting regret to pervade
the bosoms even of those who were enemies to his nation, and excited the just indignation of
all toward his inhuman and barbarous murderers. The blood of the great Cornstalk and of
his gallant son was mingled with the dust, but their memory is not lost in oblivion.—*Drake's
"Indians of North America," Book V., p. 49.*

and that Connoly's conduct was continually the reverse—even outrageously insulting him while under the immediate orders of Dunmore himself; secondly, we find Dunmore acting with duplicity and deception with Colonel Lewis and his brigade from Augusta county; * thirdly, we find Captain Cresap's name foisted into Logan's pretended speech, when it is evident, as we shall hereafter prove, that no names at all were mentioned in the original speech made for Logan; fourthly, it appears pretty plainly that much pains was taken by Dunmore at the treaty of Chillicothe to attach the Indian chiefs to his person, as appears from facts that afteward appeared; fifthly, the last speech from Dunmore to Captain White-eyes and the other Indian chiefs, sent in Connoly's letter to Gibson; to all which we may add his Lordship's nap of sleep while Cresap was stating his complaints against Connoly, and all Connoly's strange and unaccountable letters to Cresap.

I say, from all which it will appear that Dunmore had his views, and those views hostile to the liberties of America, in his proceedings with the Indians in the war of 1774. And the circumstances of the times, in connection with his equivocal conduct, lead us almost naturally to infer that he knew pretty well what he was about; and among other things, that he knew a war with the Indians at this time would materially subserve the views and interests of Great Britain, and consequently he perhaps might feel it a duty to promote said war; and if not, why betray such extreme solicitude to single out some conspicuous character and make him the scape-goat to bear all the blame of this war, that he and his friend Connoly might escape?

* So says Doddridge.

CHAPTER V.

The famous Logan speech examined and refuted.

It is not the smallest misfortune entailed upon the fallen sons and daughters of Adam, that the unhallowed flame of hatred and misanthropy seems to have consumed all that milk of human kindness, benevolence and love, originally planted in the heart of man in his primeval state. Hence we find—and every day's experience and a thousand facts confirm it—that one of the strongest propensities of human nature is to search out and expose the failings of our brethren. A thousand good, great and noble actions pass in review before us daily, unnoticed, and sink into oblivion, while the smallest deviation from the more rigid rules of propriety is presented before the public for scorn and derision. So true it is that we are eagle-eyed to see the mote in our brother's eye, when behold! a beam is in our own.

It is not, however, my business at present to inquire after the beams in the eyes of the Philosopher of Monticello and the pious Dr. Doddridge, but to remove, if I can, the mote from the eye of Captain Cresap.

He stands charged by the former with the murder of Logan's (the Indian) family on Yellow Creek, and with being infamous for his many Indian murders. Heavy charges. And by the latter with being the cause of Dunmore's war of 1774.

These, we grant, are heavy charges; and supported, or attempted to be supported, by witnesses of the first respectability. If, then, these facts can be proved and sustained, there can be no question that my client must be condemned;

but may it please this honorable court and jury (I mean all the world) to suspend their decision for one half-hour. I hope in that time to satisfy them that all these charges, whatever may be the blackness of their present aspect, are but the visions of fancy, the offspring of hasty credulity, and as flippant and unsubstantial as the quivering gossamer of a Summer's day.

But to avoid confusion, we will take up the several counts in the indictment in the order they stand, and devote this chapter to an examination of the charges offered by the first witness, *i. e.*, Mr. Jefferson; and as there are two counts in this charge we will attend to each in due order.

But, may it please the court, it is my duty before we enter into a discussion as to the truth or falsity of the charges in the indictment, to enter my protest and file a bill of exceptions to the competency of this witness; first, because we say his residence was several hundred miles from the scene of action, either where Logan's family were killed, or where and when this pretended speech was delivered; secondly, because his testimony is *hearsay* testimony, and therefore inadmissible in any legal court—which the witness himself, as a lawyer, will not deny; thirdly, as to the second item in his charge, we say the accuser, Mr. Jefferson, never saw nor had any acquaintance with the accused, Captain Cresap; nor do we believe he ever heard any man, woman or child say that Captain Cresap was a man "*infamous for his many Indian murders;*" and if he did, it was hearsay testimony again, and is good for nothing.

But inasmuch as a great many respectable members of this court are now absent, and scattered all over this vast continent, and it is more than probable that they have already decided on this case on an *ex-parte* hearing, I must take the liberty of entering into an argument upon the merits of the question, in hopes of obtaining a reversal of judgment.

The leading and most important fact in this case is, may it please your honors, that Logan never made any speech* at all ; and if he did, he told an absurd, willful and wicked lie. But we say he never made any speech—at least, not the speech in question; neither was he at the treaty of Chillicothe, where it is said this pretended speech was delivered; and fortunately we have indubitable living testimony to this fact, from a gentleman of unimpeachable veracity, which the reader shall see in the appendix.   But, as this is the first and perhaps most important link in the chain, it is proper the reader should have it in detail.

It appears, then, that while preparations were making for the treaty of Chillicothe, in the autumn of the year 1774, Simon Girty, an Indian interpreter, was sent by the Earl of Dunmore to Logan's town to invite him to the treaty; that Benjamin Tomlinson, Esq., one of Dunmore's officers, was then on the out-guard; that as Girty was passing by him he stopped and conversed some time with him; that he told Mr. Tomlinson his business, but said he did not like it, for that Logan was a surly fellow, &c.; that after the treaty had commenced, and when he was officer of the day to preserve order, he saw Simon Girty return; that a circle or ring was immediately formed around him; that Logan was not with him, nor did he come to the treaty; that John Gibson,† who was in the

---

* Of the *genuineness of that speech* nothing need be said.   It was known to the camp where it was delivered; *it was given out by Lord Dunmore and his officers :* it ran through the public papers of these States ; was rehearsed *as an exercise at schools ; published in the papers and periodical works of Europe;* and all this a dozen years before it was copied into the *Notes on Virginia.   In fine, General Gibson concludes the question forever, by declaring that he received it from Logan and delivered it to Lord Dunmore,* and that the copy in the Notes is a faithful copy.—*Appendix to Jefferson's Notes,* p. 265.

†John Gibson has always been regarded as an honest and truthful person.   He enjoyed the confidence of Washington, who, in 1781, entrusted him with the command of the Western Military Department.   In 1782, when Gen. Irvine had succeeded him, Col. Gibson was en-

ring, took Simon Girty aside, and after conversing a little while in private, he saw Gibson go into a tent and soon after return with a piece of new, clean paper in his hand, on which was written a speech from Logan. "As I stood," says Mr. Tomlinson, "near Dunmore's person, I heard this speech read three times—once by Gibson and twice by Dunmore; but neither was the name of Cresap nor any other name mentioned in this speech. I then saw Dunmore put the speech among the treaty papers."

Now here, may it please the court, is a witness unimpeached and unimpeachable, and fully competent to bear testimony, who declares, first, that Logan was not at the treaty; that the pretended speech was made by Gibson, whose sensibility, perhaps, was a little wounded by the loss of his squaw, who was Logan's sister, and unhappily killed at Yellow creek; nor yet was Cresap's name in the speech.

I ask then, where shall we look, or where is the man, that can unriddle this mystery? To charge this interpolation upon Mr. Jefferson seems not fair, because we have no evidence of the fact; to say that it was in the original is most manifestly untrue, not only from the testimony of Mr. Tomlinson, but from the certainty that so malicious and unjust a charge against Captain Cresap in his own presence, and not only in his own presence, but in the presence of at least five hundred persons, who all well know, from personal knowledge, that Captain Cresap had no more concern nor connection with the affairs at Yellow creek than Mr. Jefferson himself. I say then, that it is impossible that it

trusted with the command during the General's absence, which continued for several mouths. Jefferson, Madison and Harrison respected him. He was a Major General of Militia, Secretary of Indian Territory under the administration of Jefferson and Madison; member of the Pennsylvania Convention in 1778; and an Associate Judge of the Court of Common Pleas of Alleghany County, Pa. Chief Justice Gibson and General George Gibson, sons of Colonel Gibson who was mortally wounded at St. Clair's defeat, are his well known and esteemed nephews.—*Brantz Mayer's Address*, p. 80.

should be in the original, because the lie would have been detected and exposed upon the spot.

The only rational way that occurs to my mind to solve this difficulty is to suppose that Dunmore—or Connoly, after he joined Dunmore, with a view to throw the blame of this war on Cresap, and divert the public attention from themselves—copied this Gibson-Logan speech,* and inserted the name of Cresap; and that this copy, by some means, came to the hands of Mr. Jefferson. If not so, there is an inexplicable secret in this business that nothing but the light of Eternal Justice can ever develope.

Had Mr. Jefferson stopped at this point, we have ourselves hammered out an excuse for him; but what shall we say to the more dreadful charge against Cresap, of being a man *"infamous for his many Indian murders."* It is well Captain Cresap did not live to hear this story; if he had, alas! alas!

Gentle reader, I have given you an honest, complete and faithful detail of all the affairs Captain Cresap ever had with the Indians, and I know that I am sufficiently acquainted with his whole history, to declare that nothing is hid; nothing behind the curtain. Where then do we find, in all his proceedings against these people any one fact or circumstance that will warrant such a charge as this; and I beseech you, where in the name of common sense, of justice, mercy, truth, or that common civility due from man to man, could our honorable ex-president find a motive to publish to the world, and all succeeding generations, a charge so odious and detestable.

---

*In respect to the speech of Logan, it would be highly gratifying if a few matters connected with it could be settled; but whether they ever will, time only can determine. From the statement of Dr. Barton, we are led to expect that he had other documents than those he at that time published, going to show that Cresap was not the murderer of Logan's family, but he never published them, as I can learn, and he has left us to conjecture upon such as we have.—*Druke's Fifth Book of the Indians, p.* 48.

I take it for granted, that no honest historian will record facts equivocal and doubtful and hand them down to posterity for truth, with the imposing sanction of their own celebrity. If then, Mr. Jefferson had heard stories of Captain Cresap (which we are under the impression he never did), yet if it was, it was vague report, unsubstantiated by any evidence, because it was not true.

And I ask, what would this honorable gentleman think, were we to measure to him the same measure he has meted to Cresap? We also have heard stories about him, but as we know but little as to their truth, we let them sleep.

Yet certainly it is the best for those who dwell in glass houses not to throw stones. But before we dismiss this subject, I must be permitted to return to a remark long since made, namely, that my task is extremely difficult.

To prove a negative, and especially a negative so indefinite as not to apply to any particular or specific period, is more difficult still. For instance, A charges B with stealing a horse, but does not say of whom, where nor when; now, I pray you, how is B to meet and refute a charge of this kind? But again, A charges B with stealing a horse from D, on the night of August 20th, 1820, out of D's stable, in the town of Wheeling; now in this case a negative can be proven, because B can prove that on the first day of August, and for many preceding and succeeding days he was in the city of Baltimore. So here is positive proof against positive proof, and the credibility of the witness will decide it. But the first case is the case before us. Captain Cresap is charged with being infamous for many Indian murders; now this charge embraces his whole life, and is of that vague, shapeless, and indefinite kind that it is impossible to bring testimony to bear upon it, unless we could prove where he was and what he was about every day of his life, from about ten years old until his death.

But it is our duty and our business to deny the charge in toto, and call upon the accuser to prove it. Here then we rest the subject, until these charges are put into some shape or specific form. We trust they will sink with all general charges of the kind, into the dark shades of oblivion, and where also the names and characters of the accuser and accused must shortly go.*

---

*This was written in March, 1824, since which, the answer has also gone to the accused. August 28, 1826.

CHAPTER VI.

Doctor Doddridge's Book—Charge against Captain Cresap examined and refuted.

Having had the honor of traveling so long with one of the ex-Presidents of the United States, we part by mutual consent, and I trust in good humor, at least it is so on my part. I now turn round to face my old friend, the Rev. Dr. Doddridge; and is it true, that this herald of the gospel of peace and good will to men; this son of the West—who can not but be perfectly acquainted with the nature of savage warfare, and who has, I believe, seen, and heard, and felt some of its effects—who ought not to have forgotten the efforts made by Captain Cresap to defend the frontier at this perilous season, and that among those exposed families, his father's was one; and is it, I say, or can it be true, that this reverend Doctor, like another Brutus, raises his consecrated and hallowed hand to give another stab to wounded Cæsar?

And why and wherefore is this, Doctor? Did you think it a duty incumbent upon you, as a faithful historian, to state facts of a vague, equivocal and doubtful nature, merely to swell the pages of your history? or were you of opinion that the name of a man so well known and so conspicuous a character as Captain Cresap would embellish your discrepant narrative? But whatever may have been your motive, nothing will justify a departure from truth in a historian; for, although were we to admit that a writer is not bound to say everything he knows respecting a character he attempts to narrate, yet he is certainly bound to say nothing at random, or what he does not know.

9

Doctor Beattie says, when we doubt a man's word, we have always one of these four reasons : 1st. We think that what he says is incredible or improbable. 2d. There is some temptation or motive which inclines him in the present case to violate truth. 3d. That he is not a competent judge of the matter wherein he gives testimony. 4th. We doubt his veracity now because we have known him to be a deceiver formerly.

And he says again, that of a person of whom we know nothing, modesty requires that we should say nothing; and candor at least requires that we should say nothing abusive.

But Dr. Doddridge not only says a great deal about Captain Cresap, of whom he never knew anything, for I suppose he was dead before Doddridge was born ; but he also violates most egregiously Dr. Beattie's other rule, namely : by abusing him most unmercifully.

But he (Beattie) gives us four reasons for doubting testimony, one of which, and the most innocent I believe of the four is, that the testifier is an incompetent judge of the matter wherein or whereof he gives testimony. Now as we know, and are confident, that Dr. Doddridge has given us, to say the least, a most incorrect and uncandid statement of the cause of Dunmore's war, and of the proceedings of Captain Cresap about the time that war commenced, hence, we will for charity's sake attribute the incorrect statement, made by the Doctor, to a want of competency to judge and report of facts with which he could not in the nature of the things have any knowledge ; at least no other knowledge than mere vague report, or perhaps vain conjecture. But what is most strange in this business is, that Dr. Doddridge himself acknowledges in his preface how imperfect his acquaintance is with this part of his history.

But to proceed. Doddridge says (page 225), *"devoutly might*

humanity wish that the record of the causes which led to the de-
structive war of 1774, *might be blotted from the annals of our*
country;" and permit me to retort, that it is most devoutly to
be wished, that a minister of the everlasting gospel had not
been the first to commit to record a string of assumed facts,
upon no better authority, and thus to register in the annals of
our country what never appeared before in any record ; *most*
devoutly is it to be wished, might the Doctor say, that I could
some way or another, have avoided, or been restrained from,
uttering what I do not know to be true ; and I now call upon
the Doctor to produce those records in the annals of our
country which he says is now too late to efface.

How passing strange is this! what affected sensibility for
the honor of our country! when at the same time—so far as
the honor of our country is involved in the causes leading to
Dunmore's war, he himself, even Dr. Doddridge has used his
best endeavors, by laying before the public and the world,
a statement of *false facts* (I have Jefferson's authority for
these words), and giving such erroneous views of the real
causes of Dunmore's war, that if the honor of our country
suffers it must be through his means, and for the want of
correct information.

But, inasmuch as I have in my IV chapter given the reader
what I think is a faithful and correct view of the causes leading to the war of 1774, and not from vague report or conjecture, but from personal memory and many records, it is,
therefore, I presume, needless to repeat and say over again
what has already been said; and I trust, that personal knowledge of facts aided and frequently confirmed by records, will
be deemed sufficient testimony to outweigh the credibility of
a story told from hearsay fifty years after all the facts and
circumstances have laid buried in oblivion.

But the Doctor says (page 266), that a certain report of the Indians stealing horses—which report, he says, was not true, but I say it was true, although of little importance—*yet that report, vague as it was, induced a pretty general belief that the Indians were about to make war upon the frontier settlements, but for this apprehension there does not appear to be the slightest foundation.*

Now all this is wonderful—passing wonderful—for either Dr. Doddridge did know, or did not know, of some of the material facts connected with the beginning of this war, to-wit: Connoly's* circular letter; the white men killed by the Indians on Hocking, in 1773, and the two men killed in Butler's canoe about the first of May, 1774; the unceasing hostilities between the Indians and whites in Kentucky, and the general panic among all the settlements in the western country, and their running into forts about the last of April. Now if the Doctor knows all this, and has suppressed it, he is bound to account with the public and the world for such a material omission. But if he did not know these facts—most of which are matters of record—it proves to absolute demonstration his incompetency and ignorance of the most material facts connected with the history he undertakes to write. But his own history confutes itself; for I ask if any man in his senses can believe, that a mere idle

---

* On the 21st of April, Connoly wrote to the settlers along the Ohio, that the Shawanese were not to be trusted, and that they (the whites) ought to be prepared to revenge any wrong done them. Five days before its date, a canoe, belonging to William Butler, a leading Pittsburg trader, had been attacked by three Cherokees, and one white man had been killed. This happened not far from Wheeling, and became known there of course; while about the same time the report was general that the Indians were stealing the traders' horses. When, therefore, immediately after Connoly's letter had been circulated, the news came to that settlement that some Indians were coming down the Ohio in a boat, Cresap, in revenge for the murder by the Cherokees, and as he afterward said, in obedience to the direction of the commandant at Pittsburg, contained in the letter referred to, determined to attack them. They were, as it chanced, two friendly Indians, who, with two whites, had been dispatched by William Butler, when he heard his first messengers were stopped, to attend to his peltries down the river, in the Shawanee country.—*Perkins's Annals of the West, page* 123.

and doubtful report of the Indians stealing horses, as he states it, would have had the effect of putting a whole country, at least sixty miles square, into such a panic and alarm as to fly into forts, which he knows was the fact; and we also know, that the Indians as well as the white people, often stole horses from our frontiers in peace as well as in war.

But that the Indians did actually steal horses from Mr. Joseph Tomlinson, at Grave creek; and Mr. Richard Mc Macken, a little below Wheeling, about this time, is most certain; yet this was a very inconsiderable item in the causes leading to Dunmore's war.

Having premised thus much, we pronounce beforehand, that the Doctor's book will not bear the scrutiny of being judged by these rules, (the rules laid down by Dr. Beattie, and also by myself), because none of the charges he brings against Captain Cresap stand upon any better testimony than his mere *say so*, and this *say so* proof is unsupported by any direct or inferential evidence. Hence it appears that they all originated in himself.

But we will do the Doctor ample justice, and pay him the respect of traveling, however tedious and irksome our journey may be, through all his charges, taking them in the order they rise, admitting what is truth—if we find any —and exposing and refuting what is most assuredly untrue.

The Doctor's first charge is general, and like one we have lately discussed, not susceptible of direct proof against it, to-wit: *that Captain Cresap was the cause of Dunmore's war;* but he has also superadded several specific and direct charges, which are consequently more in our power to controvert.

I believe his first specific assertion, bearing on this subject, that deserves our notice is, that the white people shed the first blood in the war of 1774; or, in other words, began the war.

Secondly: He says Captain Cresap commanded the Fort at Wheeling.

Thirdly: He charges Captain Cresap with the murder of two Indians in a canoe, and goes on to say, that afterward on the same day, he went down to Capteening and had a battle with some more.

Fourthly: He says Colonel Zane expostulated with Captain Cresap before he attacked the Indians in the canoe, but that he would not regard him.

Fifthly: He says the massacre on Yellow Creek, and battle at Capteening, comprehended all the family of Logan, meaning, I suppose, that they were all killed at these two places.

Sixthly: He calls Colonel Lewis General Lewis, and Logan* a Cyuga chief; whereas, he was a Mingo, and no chief.

Seventhly: He says the authenticity of Logan's speech is no longer a subject of doubt.

Eighthly: Logan, he says, sent his speech in a belt of wampum.

I believe the foregoing affords us an analysis of all the general and specific charges in Doddridge's book against Captain Cresap. We shall therefore now take them up in the order they stand.

---

* SIMON KENTON, who was taken prisoner by the savages, spent two nights with his captors and Logan on the head waters of the Scioto. "Well, young man," said Logan addressing Kenton, the night of his arrival, "these chaps seem very mad with you.' "Yes," replied Kenton, "they appear so." "But don't be disheartened," interrupted Logan, "I am a great chief; you are to go to Sandusky; they talk of *burning* you there; but I will send two runners to-morrow to *speak good* for you!" And so he did, for on the morrow, having detained the hostile party, he dispatched the promised envoys to Sandusky, though he did not report to Kenton of their success when they returned at nightfall. The runners, by Logan's orders, interceded with Captain Druyer, an influential British Indian-agent at Sandusky, who with great difficulty ransomed the prisoner and saved him from the brutal sacrifice of the stake.—*Discourse by Brantz Mayer, p.* 66.

And first, as to the general charge that Captain Cresap was the author of Dunmore's war. Now, although we have admitted, and do admit, the difficulty of answering this broad, vague and indefinite charge, yet I trust we shall be able to offer stronger reasons against the truth of it than he has or can produce for it.

In the first place, then, we believe, and are convinced, that no man,* red, white or black, ever heard of this charge before, either in English, Indian, Dutch, French, Latin, Greek or Hebrew, in the whole course of about fifty years, to-wit: from the year 1774 to 1824; hence we are led to the inevitable conclusion that this charge is *bran span* new—just hatched in a parson's cap in Wellsburg. I therefore deny the charge, and call upon Dr. Doddridge for the proof, either from certain and indisputable testimony, or from any genuine record of the transactions of the day; and until he does so, I give this charge to the winds, or throw it back with all its malignity upon himself, to shake off if he can.

Second.—We have, however, more arguments in reserve to meet and refute this charge; and I cannot but think that the candid and faithful detail I have given the reader in the fourth chapter of this work, of all the proceedings of Captain Cresap, and every circumstance in connection with the Indian war of 1774, affords one of the most weighty and forcible arguments in this case.

Third.—I ask, how comes it to pass that neither Cornstalk, head chief of the Shawanee tribe of Indians, nor any other chief of the various tribes who attended the treaty of Pittsburg, in September, of the year 1775, never once mentioned the name of Cresap as the aggressor, or cause, or beginner of

---

* I am not absolutely certain that Mr. Jefferson does not hint something like this. I have not his book before me, and it is many years since I read it.

the war of the preceding year? And this is the more remarkable as Cornstalk and the Shawanee chiefs were hard
pressed by the Virginia commission as to their compliance
with one of the articles of the treaty of Chillicothe; and this
fact happens to be matter of record, as I have before me, as
already remarked, this original treaty.

Moreover, it is stated by Captain Wood that on the 25th
day of July he arrived at the Seneca town, where he found
Logan* and several other Mingoes; that they were pretty
drunk and angry; that Logan repeated in plain English how
the *people of Virginia* had killed his mother, sister and all
his relations, during which he wept and sung alternately.
Now, may we not ask how it happened that this drunken
Indian, with his feelings highly excited, never once mentions
the name of Cresap? And may we not further remark that
this fact, which happens to be matter of record, cuts like a
two-edged sword—not only by implication giving the lie to
his pretended speech, but affording at the same time an argument that whatsoever might be the opinion of their advocate,
Dr. Doddridge, it was not the opinion of the Indians themselves that Cresap was the cause of Dunmore's war. But
enough.

And we now proceed to take up the Doctor's long list of
specific charges, in the order they occur.

---

* The Rev. Dr. David McClure, during a visit to Fort Pitt and the neighboring regions of
the Ohio, met our hero, and saw many other Indians who were in the habit of resorting to the
settlements for the sake of a drunken frolic, staggering about the town. At that time Logan
was still remarkable for the grandeur of his personal appearance. TAH-GAH-JUTE, or *"Short
Dress,"* for such was his Indian name, stood several inches more than six feet in hight; he
was straight as an arrow; lithe, athletic, and symmetrical in figure; firm, resolute, and commanding in feature; but the brave, open, and manly countenance he possessed in his earlier
years was now changed for one of martial ferocity. After tarrying and preaching nearly three
weeks at Fort Pitt, Dr. McClure, in the summer or autumn of 1772, set out for Muskingum,
accompanied by a Christian Indian as his interpreter. The second day after his departure, the
wayfarers unexpectedly encountered Logan. Painted and equipped for war, and accompanied
by another savage, he lurked a few rods from the path beneath a tree, leaning on his rifle; nor
did the missionary notice him until apprised by the interpreter that Logan desired to speak

The first is, that the white people began the war of 1774. Now, it is evident that if we were to admit its truth, it would not apply to Captain Cresap more than any other man ; but, interwoven and connected with the thread of his history, he appears to wish it to be understood as applying to Cresap. But as I have already proved in my fourth chapter—not from assertion only, but from authentic documents—that this assertion is not true, and that it rests upon no better authority than the parson's *ipse dixit*, we need not weary the reader's patience by multiplying arguments or using repetition in this case.

The Doctor's second assertion is, that " *Captain Cresap commanded Fort Wheeling at the commencement of the war.*" Now this charge, considered as detached from inferences and consequences, would seem to mean nothing, nor have any tendency to injure the character of Cresap. But when we consider the adjuncts and inferences the Doctor designs we shall draw from this circumstance, it wears a serious aspect, because he intends we shall consider Cresap as a prowling wolf, who makes his den in Wheeling, sallying out occasionally and killing his poor sheep, the Indians ; and moreover, because the design of this assertion is to entirely mislead the mind of the public as to the real fact and circumstances that accidentally led Captain Cresap to that place at all.

---

with him. McClure immediately rode to the spot where the red man remained, and asked what he required. For a moment Logan stood pale and agitated before the preacher, and then, pointing to his breast, exclaimed : "I feel bad here. Wherever I go the evil Manethoes pursue " me. If I go into my cabin, my cabin is full of devils. If I go into the woods, the trees and " the air are full of devils. They haunt me by day and by night. They seem to want to " catch me, and throw me into a deep pit, full of fire." In this moody strain of abrupt, maudlin musing—with the unnatural pallor still pervading his skin—he leant for awhile on his rifle, and continued to brood over the haunting devils. At length he broke forth with an earnest appeal to the missionary as to "what he should do?" Dr. McClure gave him sensible and friendly advice suggested by the occasion ; counselled him to reflect on his past life ; considered him as weighed down by remorse for the errors or cruelties of past years, and exhorted him to that sincere penitence and prayer which would drive from him the "evil Manethoes" forever. —*Brantz Mayer's Address*, p. 32.

I have already stated, in my third and fourth chapters, the real and true state of this case—namely: that Captain Cresap, being warned of his danger, fled to Fort Wheeling as a place of refuge; that he was a mere bird of passage—a transient (though I believe very welcome) guest; that he had no more right to assume the command of Fort Wheeling than a traveler, who may call and tarry a night with any of you gentlemen, has to assume the command of your family and servants; and that in fact he tarried there but a few days, as he was, perhaps, at this time dependent upon the hospitality of his friend Colonel Zane, who was the real commandant.

Third.—But the Doctor has more yet against us, and of a more serious nature—namely: *that Captain Cresap killed two Indians in a canoe.*

I have already admitted that two Indians were killed in a canoe—not by Captain Cresap personally, but two of his men; and we also admit that some of the English red-coats were killed at Lexington by some wicked Yankees, in April, 1775. Now, in the former case, we have shown that it was subsequent to acts of hostility by the Indians, and at a time when war was considered as inevitable, and as actually begun. But in the latter case, the red-coats and the Yankees went at it pell mell, and both were the first aggressors; yet who ever blamed our Yankees for this?

But, as I have already anticipated and answered the Doctor as to this charge, in my fourth chapter, I need not add any more here. But the Doctor adds, that after Captain Cresap killed the two Indians in the canoe, he went down the Ohio the same day, and killed more Indians at the mouth of Capteening. So, then, this prowling wolf having killed two Indians—*up the river*, the Doctor says, but he does not say how far up—*yet insatiable*, passed by his den and went down the river about fifteen or eighteen miles the same day, and killed more. Now this story contradicts itself; 'tis scarcely possible that any men could do this without the aid of swift horses or a balloon, neither of which I suppose they had. But I have also given the reader a candid and honest statement of this fact in my fourth chapter, therefore need not repeat it again and again.

Fourth.—But Colonel Zane, says the Doctor, "*expostulated with Captain Cresap about killing the two Indians.*" We deny this assertion, and call on his reverence to prove it—and not by assertion or vague report, but positively and pointedly; because we conceive this charge the mere offspring of malevolence, and designed to present Captain Cresap before the public in the most odious colors.

Fifth.—He tells us that *the massacre on Yellow Creek and the battle on Capteening comprehended all the family of Logan*—meaning, I presume, that all Logan's family were killed at those two places. Now, that several of Logan's family were killed at Yellow Creek we never heard disputed, but that any part of that family was killed at Capteening we never heard before; and we have seen in the preceding pages of this work that only one Indian was killed there, or in the skirmish Cresap had with the Indians on the Ohio—whether at Capteening or elsewhere is uncertain; but who this Indian was, or of what family, I know not, nor ever heard; nor can any reason be offered why these two affairs of Yellow Creek and Capteening should be thus blended together, except that the Doctor is determined in some way or other to lug in Captain Cresap as one of the murderers of Logan's family.*

---

* John Sappington states that he was "intimately acquainted with all the circumstances respecting the destruction of Logan's family," though he does not admit, in his carefully drawn statement, that he was *present* at the scene of murder. McKee, in his certificate appended to Sappington's testimony in Jefferson's Notes, says that Sappington admitted he was the man who

But, if we were to admit that this Indian killed at Capteening was in fact one of Logan's family, it would neither
add nor diminish aught to the innocence or criminality of the
action. The only conceivable motive for blending the two
affairs of Yellow Creek and Capteening, is to give a kind of
currency to the Logan speech; for we shall presently see that
the Doctor himself is constrained to acknowledge, although
indirectly and covertly, yet plainly enough, that Captain
Cresap was not, nor had he any agency or concern in the
affair on Yellow Creek.

Sixth.—The Doctor calls Colonel Lewis General Lewis, and
Logan a Cayuga chief—in both of which he is incorrect; nor
is it of any other importance than to show a want of precision
and accuracy in his history, that may lead to suspicion in
matters of greater importance; and that the Doctor is mistaken in the grade of Colonel Lewis is most certain, because,
before our Revolutionary war, Virginia had in her militia no
higher military grade than county lieutenant with the title of
colonel; and that he is also mistaken respecting his favorite,
the grand Indian orator, Prince Logan, appears not only from
the certificate of Benjamin Tomlinson, Esq., but also from
Captain Wood's journal.

Seventh.—He says the authenticity of the Logan speech *is
now no longer a subject of doubt;* and for fear the reader should
be so unhappy as to die without being gratified with such a
delicious feast, he gives him the whole speech.

---

killed Logan's brother. See also the statement written by Mr. Jolly, published in the American Journal of Science and Art, vol. xxxi, p. 10.

It is important to recollect that all these statements and depositions positively prove that
Captain Michael Cresap was neither present at nor countenanced the alleged murder of Logan's
kin at the Yellow Creek massacre. The fact that Sappington's statement was published by Mr.
Jefferson himself, indicates the confidence he placed in it, especially as he inserts it as a sort of
supplement to the other testimony on the subject which had been printed before its reception.
Logan's mother, brother and sister, (Gibson's Indian wife or squaw, in all likelihood,) were,
probably, all of the relatives of Logan killed there.—*Brantz Mayer's Address, p.* 53.

Now, gentle reader, I do most earnestly entreat your patience while I endeavor, with all simplicity, to bring into your view this crooked and unparalleled jumble of contradictions. Let us see how this story will hang together:

1. We are told that there is now no longer any doubt as to the authenticity of this Logan speech, and of course, I presume he means to say, the facts contained in that speech—one of which most prominent facts, according to the speech as recited by himself, is that Colonel Cresap, the last Spring, in cold blood and unprovoked, murdered all Logan's relations, not even sparing his women and children.

2. He says the *massacre* at Capteening, and that which took place at Baker's,* about forty miles above Wheeling, a few days after that at Capteening, were unquestionably the sole cause of the war of 1774. The last was perpetrated by thirty-two men under the command of Daniel Greathouse. The whole number killed at the place, and on the river opposite, was twelve, &c., &c.

Now, here is an artful, dark, and yet sufficiently explicit confession that Captain Cresap had no concern in the Yellow Creek business, or in killing Logan's relations; yet it is told in such ambiguous and indistinct terms, as it should seem purposely to deceive the reader; for, instead of telling us plainly that this affair at Baker's was in fact the affair of

---

* Baker was a man who sold rum, and the Indians had made frequent visits at his house, induced probably by their fondness for that liquor. He had been particularly desired by Cresap to remove and take away his rum, and he was actually preparing to move at the time of the murder. The evening before a squaw came over to Baker's house, and by her crying seemed to be in great distress. The cause of her uneasiness being asked, she refused to tell; but getting Baker's wife alone, she told her that the Indians were going to kill her and all her family the next day, that she loved her, did not wish her to be killed, and therefore told her what was intended, that she might save herself. In consequence of this information, Baker got a number of men, to the amount of twenty-one, to come to his house, and they were all there before morning. A council was held, and it was determined that the men should lie concealed in the back apartment; that if the Indians did come and behaved themselves peaceably, they should not be molested; but if not, the men were to show themselves and act accordingly. Early in the morning seven Indians, four men and three squaws, came over. Logan's brother was one

10

Yellow Creek, and that the people that were killed there were Logan's relations, he has put the statement of this fact into such a shape as no doubt to have deceived his readers, with the meritorious view of saving the Logan speech and vilifying most cruelly and unjustly the character of Captain Cresap. And what makes this suspicion stronger is, he calls the battle at Capteening (for he will have a battle there, right or wrong,) a "massacre;" whereas I have shown, and I hope satisfactorily, too, that there was no more reason to call that battle a massacre than Lewis's battle at the mouth of Kanawha, or any other battle fought during the whole war. Nor do I believe, from everything I have heard—although I am far from advocating this Yellow Creek business of murdering women in cool blood—yet I say from all I have ever heard of this business, that the Doctor has given a tolerably correct and honest statement of that affair; certainly he is wrong in a most essential point, for the Yellow Creek business was antecedent to that at Capteening, and is entirely distinct, and has no connection with it.

But the wonderful part of this story yet remains to be told, and it plainly comes out to be Doddridge *versus* Doddridge; for first he tells us that the authenticity of the Logan speech is now no longer a subject of doubt, that this authentic speech

---

of them. They immediately got rum, and all, except Logan's brother, became very much intoxicated. At this time all the men were concealed, except the man of the house, Baker, and two others, who staid out with him. Those Indians came unarmed. After some time Logan's brother took down a coat and hat belonging to Baker's brother-in-law, who lived with him, and put them on, and setting his arms akimbo, began to strut about, till at length coming up to one of the men, he attempted to strike him, saying, "*white man son of a bitch.*" The white man, whom he treated thus, kept out of his way for some time, but growing irritated he jumped to his gun, and shot the Indian as he was making to the door with the coat and hat on him. The men who lay concealed then rushed out and killed the whole of them, excepting one child, which I believe is alive yet. But before this happened, two canoes, one with two, the other with five Indians, *all naked, painted, and armed completely for war*, were discovered to start from the shore on which Logan's camp was. Had it not been for this circumstance, the white men would not have acted as they did; but this confirmed what the squaw had told before. The white men having killed as aforesaid the Indians in the house, ranged themselves along

gives us clear and unequivocal testimony that Colonel Cresap murdered all Logan's family at Yellow Creek, not sparing his women and children; secondly, that this family of Logan's who were killed at Baker's—which is the same place and same people—were killed by Daniel Greathouse and thirty-two men, among whom he has not, and among whom truth and his own conscience would not permit him to name Captain Cresap. So here we have Logan in a speech charging Colonel Cresap with killing his relations, and a Dr. Doddridge confirming the truth of that speech with all the weight his assertion, his book and character can give it, and at the same time, in the same book and in the same chapter, acknowledging that it was not Cresap but Greathouse that committed the murder and massacre at Yellow Creek. Now, I ask the reader if he ever saw an argument so much like the letter X with the Doctor stuck on each point?

But, how shall we account for all this? Did Dr. Doddridge believe, or did he not believe that Captain Cresap killed Logan's family? If he did, and does believe it, pray who were the people killed by Greathouse? And why has he not, somewhere in his book, charged Captain Cresap with this among all his other charges? For I have nowhere yet discovered any disposition in the Doctor to spare him. But if, on the

the bank of the river to receive the canoes. The canoe with the two Indians came near, being the foremost. Our men fired upon them and killed them both. The other canoe then went back. After this two other canoes started, the one containing eleven, the other seven Indians, *painted and armed as the first.* They attempted to land below our men, but were fired upon, had one killed, and retreated, at the same time firing back. To the best of my recollection there were three of the Greathouses engaged in this business This is a true representation of the affair from beginning to end. I was intimately acquainted with Cresap, and know he had no hand in the transaction. He told me himself afterward, at Redstone Old Fort, that the day before Logan's people were killed, he, with a small party, had an engagement with a party of Indians on Capteener, about forty-four miles lower down. Logan's people were killed at the mouth of Yellow Creek, on the 24th of May, 1774; and the 23d. the day before, Cresap was engaged, as already stated. I know likewise that he was generally blamed for it, and believed by all, who were not acquainted with the circumstances, to have been the perpetrator of it. I know that he despised and hated the Greathouses ever afterward on account of it.—*Appendix to Jefferson's Notes on Virginia, p.* 266.

contrary, he did not, nor does not believe that Captain Cresap
had any concern in this Yellow Creek massacre, why does he
attempt to palm the Logan speech on the public for a genuine,
authentic document?—knowing in his own conscience that if
the speech itself is authentic, it is an authentic record of lies,
which he was bound in honor, as an honest man, and in candor and veracity as a historian, to publish to the world.

Eighth.—But as Logan was not at the treaty, Dr. Doddridge tells us *he sent his speech in a belt of wampum;* so, right
or wrong, by hook or by crook, in some way or other, the
Doctor must have a Logan speech.

" *He sent his speech in a belt of wampum!*"

Now, if I am not greatly mistaken here is one new thing
under the sun—a perfect original. That the Indians use belts
of wampum and strings of wampum in their treaties, which
serve for them as records, and also generally at the conclusion
of their harangues or speeches, as a kind of amen or confirm-
ation, is not disputed; but a speech in a belt of wampum,
unaccompanied with a message, is quite a new thing—and in
fact a thing that never happens. The reader, by recurring to
a preceding page of this work, will see the use of belts and
strings of wampum, as well from the English and French
officers at Detroit, the Delaware tribe of Indians, as from the
said Delawares to Captain Wood, and from Captain Wood to
them; but we do not find that in either instance these belts
became vocal; on the contrary, they were as quiescent and
silent as a dormouse.

But as the speech of the Delaware chiefs to Captain Wood
is not very long, and may serve as a specimen of Indian
speeches and customs, we give it to the reader, as follows:

" *Brothers the Big-knife:* Your brothers, the Delawares, are
"very thankful to you for your good talk yesterday, and are

"glad to find their brothers' hearts are good toward them, "and they will be joyful at meeting them at the time and "place you mention.

"Brothers, in order to convince our elder brothers of Vir- "ginia that we desire to live in friendship with them, I now "deliver to you this *belt and string;* they were sent to us by "an Englishman and a Frenchman [in a subsequent meeting Captain Wood had with the Wyandots, they denied that the French had any concern in this business, but that it was the English only,] at Detroit, with a *message* that the people of "Virginia were determined to strike us; that they would "come upon us two different ways—the one by the lakes and "the other by the Ohio—and that the Virginians were deter- "mined to drive us off and to take our lands; that we must "be constantly on our guard, and not give any credit to what- "ever you said, as you were a people not to be depended "upon; that the Virginians would invite us to a treaty, but "we must not go at any rate; and to take particular notice of "the advice they gave, which proceeded from motives of real "friendship, and nothing else."

They then delivered the belt and string received from De- troit. I trust the reader now sees and understands the use made by Indians and those concerned in Indian affairs of belts of wampum. They are among these people significant symbols of peace and war, and commemorative of conditions and arti- cles of treaty. But to send a speech in a belt of wampum, unaccompanied with a message, is a thing never known. We find the message from Detroit to the Indians accompanied with a belt and string of black wampum; this was significant, and agreeable to Indian customs, and denoted war. We find, also, Captain Wood delivers a string of white wampum; this we know was emblematical of peace and good will.

I have taken more pains to elucidate this subject than, perhaps, was necessary. But as it was the last fibre in the Doctor's cobweb, I thought it best, with the brush of plain, simple, honest truth, to dash it all away together. But, before I dismiss the Doctor and conclude this chapter, may we not ask this sensitive, this tender-hearted and noble champion and defender of the Indians, where was his sympathy for the christian Delaware Indians that were massacred in cold blood by hundreds? It is true he speaks with horror of the action, but finds an apology for the perpetrators; be it so; I feel no wish to disturb the ashes of the dead, or irritate old sores that time and oblivion have buried; and only mention the circumstance to show with what avidity he seized every idle report to aid him in consigning to infamy and detestation a character which duty, gratitude, and the best feelings of the noblest mind ought to have urged him rather to eulogize. It is remarkable that Dr. Doddridge closes his chapter on the massacre of the Moravian Indians in the following words—*i. e.*, that the names of these murderers should not stain the pages of history, from his pen, at least. (Page 265.)

Alas, sir, what have you done? You have used your best endeavors to hand down to succeeding generations the name and character of a man with whom you had no acquaintance, as the most odious, the most detestable; and so far as your book and influence extends, you no doubt intended they should have this effect.

In the name, then, of that awful being whose minister you are, or ought to be, in the name of truth, justice and mercy, I ask what reparation, what atonement can you make?—not to the manes of Captain Cresap only, but to his large, extensive and respectable family, who never did nor ever wished to injure you.

CHAPTER VII.

Concluding scenes of Captain Cresap's life—marches to Boston —taken sick in camp—makes an effort to get home—dies at New York.

As a traveler worn down with weariness and fatigue looks forward with joyful and pleasing anticipations of ease and rest at his journey's end, so my weary hands and aching head are cheered as they approximate the end of toil and labor, now full in view.

Although we have repeatedly mentioned the name of Captain Cresap on various occasions in the course of our history, yet we left him personally at the conclusion of our third chapter, to which the present may properly be considered a supplement.

It was there stated, that Captain Cresap was engaged at the commencement of Dunmore's war in improving lands on the Ohio; that, being driven by the hostile attitude of our affairs with the Indians from the business he was engaged in, he took an active part in that war, and never after attended to his own business until after its conclusion. But the concluding scene, however, of this story, this chequered drama of life, remains yet to be told.

After the treaty of Chillicothe, and the army was disbanded, Captain Cresap returned to his family, and spent the latter part of the Autumn of 1774 and succeeding Winter in repose in his domestic circle—a thing, by the by, not very common with him. But very early in the Spring of 1775 he hired another set of young men and returned to the Ohio, with the

view of finishing the work he had commenced the year before.
Nor did he stop at this time at his old station on that river,
but descended with a part of his hands as low as Kentucky,
where he also made many improvements; but being indis-
posed, he left his hands and started for home. However, this
eventful period scattered again all his golden dreams, as we
shall presently see. American blood was shed, the battle of
Lexington had taken place, and all America was in a flame;
Congress had met, conventions were formed, and committees
were appointed in every section of the country; and a letter
was addressed by the delegates from Maryland in Congress
to the committee of Frederick county, requesting them with
all convenient speed to raise two companies of riflemen, &c.

But, as this letter is an important document, and naturally
leads the mind back and gives us a view into those times that
tried men's souls, and moreover as I am not sure that it has
a place in any record, I give it to the reader at full length:

"PHILADELPHIA, June 15, 1775.

"*Gentlemen:* We inclose you a resolution of Congress for
"raising two* companies of riflemen, two of which in our own
"province. It is thought this small body of men, all of which
"we expect to be expert hands, will be more serviceable for
"the defense of America in the continental army near Boston.
"You will please to observe the men are to be enlisted for
"one year, unless the affairs of America will admit of their
"discharge before that time. It is left to the delegates of
"Pennsylvania, Maryland and Virginia to fall on such meas-
"ures as may appear most likely to get the companies quickly
"formed and on their march.

"The gentlemen of Pennsylvania and Virginia write, as we

---

* It is "two" in the original, but it ought to be "six."

"do, to the committees of the counties, where it is most likely
"the best men may the soonest be had; and for the conveni-
"ence of having the whole end on all events on the same day,
"have agreed the year shall finish on the first day of July,
"1776, as we suppose the enlistments will begin about the
"first day of next month.

"The committee of your county, it is expected, will give
"recommendatory certificate of the officers for their respective
"places and ranks, and the commissions can be made out ac-
"cordingly under the direction of Congress. The companies,
"as soon as formed, will march forward to Boston with all ex-
"pedition, and it is unnecessary that there should be a rendez-
"vous of all the company at any one place before they get to
"the camp. You will, doubtless, if possible, get *experienced*
"*officers, and the very best men that can be procured, as well from*
"*your affection to the service as for the honor of our province;* we
"hope it will appear to you as to us, prudent to get the men
"as far back as may be, not only because there is a fair
"chance of their being as good as any others, but that those
"whose situations will permit, may be left at hand, to act
"in our own province, if unhappily there should be occasion,
"unless you should be advised time enough of a different
"provision. You will direct captains to give certificates of
"their necessary expenses incurred on the way for sub-
"sistence. The Virginia and Pennsylvania captains will, if
"necessary, do so too.

"We shall expect to be advised from time to time of
"the success of your endeavors, or any difficulty you may
"meet with. We have wrote to you only on this subject,
"thinking the whole may be executed in your county; but
"if you are likely to meet with any embarrassment, we
"should be glad you would speedily consult the committee

"of Baltimore, who may probably be able to render you "some assistance.

　　"We are, gentlemen,
　　　"Your most obedient servants,
　　　　　"MATTHEW TILGHMAN,
　　　　　"THOMAS JOHNSON, Jʀ.
　　　　　"JOHN HALL,
　　　　　"ROBERT GOLDSBOROUGH,
　　　　　"T. STONE,
　　　　　"WILLIAM PACA,
　　　　　"SAMUEL CHACE.
"To the Committee of Frederick County, Maryland."

In consequence of this resolve of Congress, and letter from the delegation of Maryland, the committee of Frederick immediately appointed Captain Michael Cresap and Thomas Price, of Fredericktown, captains to command these two rifle companies; and as soon as this was known, I was dispatched in all haste to give Captain Cresap notice of this appointment, and met him in the Allegheny mountains on his way. As I have already remarked, he had left his hands and business through indisposition, and was making homewards.

When I communicated my business, and announced his appointment, instead of becoming elated he became pensive and solemn, as if his spirits were really depressed; or as if he had a presentiment this was his death warrant. He said he was in bad health, and his affairs in a deranged state, but that nevertheless, as the committee had selected him, and as he understood (from me) that his father had pledged himself that he should accept of this appointment, he would go, let the consequences be what they might. He then directed me to proceed to the west side of the mountains, and publish to his old companions in arms this his intention; this I did, and in a very short time collected and brought to him, at his residence in Old Town, about twenty-two as fine fellows as ever handled a rifle, and most, if not all of them, completely equipped with rifles, etc., etc. Soon after these men joined his company, he marched,* and bid, alas! a final farewell to his family.

The immense popularity of this *"infamous Indian murderer"* will appear not only from the circumstance of twenty men marching voluntarily nearly one hundred miles—leaving their families and their all, merely from a message sent by a boy— to join the standard of their ol dcaptain ; and that, too, from the very county where, if his name was odious, it must be most odious, as being in the vicinity of those dreadful Indian murders.

But the high estimation in which Captain Cresap stood with his fellow-citizens, who certainly knew him best, will appear further from the fact, that while he was passing through the lower end of the county in which he lived, his company increased and swelled to such a multitude, that he was obliged, daily, to reject many men that wished to join his company ; and I think there is no question but that he could have raised

---

* "I have had the happiness of seeing Captain Michael Cresap marching at the head of a formidable company of upward of one hundred and thirty men from the mountains and backwoods, painted like Indians, armed with tomahawks and rifles, dressed in hunting shirts and moccasins, and though some of them had traveled near eight hundred miles from the banks of the Ohio, they seemed to walk light and easy, and not with less spirit than at the first hour of their march. Health and vigor, after what they had undergone, declared them to be intimate with hardship and familiar with danger. Joy and satisfaction were visible in the crowd that met them. Had Lord North been present, and been assured that the brave leader could raise thousands of such like to defend his country, what think you, would not the hatchet and the block have intruded on his mind ? I had an opportunity of attending the Captain during his stay in town, and watched the behavior of his men, and the manner in which he treated them ; for it seems that all who go out to war under him do not only pay the most willing obedience to him as their commander, but, in every instance of distress look up to him as their friend and father. A great part of his time was spent in listening to and relieving their wants, without any apparant sense of fatigue and trouble. When complaints were before him, he determined with kindness and spirit, and on every occasion condescended to please without losing his dignity.

"Yesterday the company were supplied with a small quantity of powder from the magazine,

a regiment, merely and chiefly from his personal influence, in less than two months; and I am clearly of opinion, that no other individual in the state of Maryland could, at that period, have raised as many men as himself.

And as a further proof of public sentiment at this period—which happens to hang on the very heels of Dunmore's war —I add a few lines, extracted from a letter written to Captain Cresap, by John Cary, a respectable citizen of Fredericktown. Mr. Cary, after speaking of some private business, concludes his letter in the following words:

" *You, and your brother soldiers, have relieved us in one quarter,* "*and our own virtue, joined with yours, is like to relieve us in the* "*other.   I wish you prosperity and happiness, and am,*
"*Yours, &c.,*

[Signed]　　　　　　　　　　　　　　　"JOHN CARY.
"*Frederick, April* 11, 1775."

The reader will permit me to remark here, that at this period, viz: immediately after the conclusion of Dunmore's war, no individual, great or small, friend or enemy, ever said, or heard it said, either that Captain Cresap murdered Logan's family or was infamous as an Indian murderer, or that he was

which wanted airing, and was not in good order for rifles; in the evening, however, they were drawn out to show the gentlemen of the town their dexterity at shooting.   A clapboard with a mark the size of a dollar, was put up; they began to fire off-hand, and the bystanders were surprised, few shots being made that were not close to or in the paper.   When they had shot for a time in this way, some lay on their backs, some on their breast or side, others ran twenty or thirty steps, and firing, appeared to be equally certain of the mark.   With this performance the company were more than satisfied, when a young man took up the board in his hand, not by the end but by the side, and holding it up, his brother walked to the distance and very coolly shot into the white; laying down his rifle, he took the board and holding it as it was held before, the second brother shot as the first had done.   By this exercise I was more astonished than pleased.   But will you believe me when I tell you that one of the men took the board, and placing it between his legs, stood with his back to a tree while another drove the centre!

"What would a regular army of considerable strength in the forests of America do with one thousand of these men, who want nothing to preserve their health and courage but water from the spring, with a little parched corn, with what they may easily procure in hunting; and who, wrapped in their blankets, in the damp of night, would choose the shade of a tree for their covering and the earth for their bed."—*Brantz Mayer's Address, p.* 63.

the cause of Dunmore's war. The two first of these charges appeared first in Jefferson's Notes, how many years after this pretended date I do not recollect; the third was hatched by Dr. Doddridge, in the hot-bed of ignorance and prejudice, about fifty years after Dunmore's war. Please pardon this digression, and we proceed.

With this first company of riflemen, although in bad health, Captain Cresap proceeded to Boston, and joined the American Army under the command of Gen. Washington; but at length admonished of his declining health, and feeling in himself, no doubt, serious forebodings of its consequences, made an effort to reach home; but finding himself too ill to proceed, stopped in the city of New York, where he ended his earthly career, on the 5th day of October, 1775, having lived a little more than thirty-three years.

Thus we are led to the concluding scene of Captain Cresap's life, than whom no man, considering the short period of his existence, ever did more for his country; and few men, since the mad-caps of Greece and Rome, have been so shamefully abused and so ungratefully treated. Captain Cresap not only sacrificed his life in defense of his country, but all his lands in Kentucky; and much of that on the Ohio was lost.

But we have seen—and indubitable facts, not to be disputed, prove it—that he died at last in the service of, and a martyr to, the liberties of his country; and we are certain that his funeral was attended with the most splendid military honors; so much so, that I myself heard a gentleman say— whether wisely or unwisely matters not—that he would not begrudge to die if his funeral could be as honorable as Cresap's.

But that no doubt may remain upon the public mind as to the estimation in which Captain Cresap stood in the year

11

1775, I take the liberty of calling their attention to the letter from the Maryland delegates in Congress to the committee of Frederick, and the proceedings of that committee in consequence thereof. We must not forget the strong and emphatic injunction in that letter to the committee, to select the most experienced officers and best men that could be procured— not only that the service required it, but that the honor of the State would also be identified with this appointment. And what was the result? Did this respectable committee of Frederick, with this injunction before their eyes and the honor of the State in their hands, appoint a man infamous as an Indian murderer, as the principal instrument and cause of the Indian war of the preceding year, yea, the murderer of the helpless women and friends of Logan in cold blood? Did this committee, I say, appoint such a man as this to the most distinguished and honorable station, in a military view, then in the gift of the State of Maryland? Can any man in his sober senses believe this? If they do, they must believe that the county of Frederick, certainly, if not the whole State of Maryland, was composed of characters the most detestable, if the best man among them was an infamous murderer. Were Cresap's accusers and defamers aware of this? Did they intend this stigma should rest not only on Frederick county, but the State at large, and indeed in some degree upon every military officer in Maryland?—because, as already remarked, Captain Cresap was the very first captain appointed in that State.

I ask a Smallwood, a Gist, a Howard, a Smith, a Williams (Williams was Lieutenant to Captain Price), how they relish the idea of such a character being preferred before them? or what is tantamount, if he had lived and continued in the army he must, according to seniority—and I hope I may now say without a blush, according to merit, also—have filled the first station and highest grade in the Maryland line. This is abundantly evident from the fact that Rawlings, who was Cresap's Lieutenant, commanded the rifle regiment that made such havoc among the Hessians who attacked Fort Washington in 1776. Thus we find his Lieutenant was promoted to a regiment in less than a year after Captain Cresap's death. Again, Williams, who was Price's Lieutenant, obtained the rank of Brigadier General before the war was over.

When the nature and date of these facts are considered, and contrasted with the loose and quite recent date* of the guess-work, malevolent, unsupported and vague charges against the character of Captain Cresap, it must appear, I think, to all men, that whatever had been the motive, or with what view, or to whatsoever end these charges were laid before the public, yet they certainly rest upon no better foundation than the baseless fabric of a vision.

We may also add, if any additional evidence is necessary to demonstrate the high estimation in which Captain Cresap stood in the year 1775, that while on his march through Frederick county, Maryland, and through all the different States, cities, towns and villages, on his way to Boston, he was hailed, caressed and honored in the highest degree, the citizens vieing with each other who should show him most respect; indeed, so much so that I was informed by one of his officers that it was his opinion that this unremitting scene of feasting and hilarity shortened his days.

---

* I do not exactly know the date of Mr. Jefferson's Notes, but am certain they were written after this period.

CHAPTER VIII.

Recapitulation, or condensed view of the whole work, to assist the reader's memory.

In my introduction, as I conceived it would be satisfactory to the reader, I have given a brief sketch of my connection and acquaintance with Captain Cresap and the Cresap family, to evince from matter of fact and substantial reason my competency—so far as a knowledge of fact was concerned—to discharge with truth and fidelity the work I undertook; and this point, I trust, is certainly gained.

My first chapter has much about the same relation to the subject and nature of my history that a corps of pioneers has to an army—namely : to clear away the brush and rubbish, but who are not designed to render any efficient service in the ranks. I have, however, presented the reader with a few hints as to the habits, customs and manners of our citizens in 1774–'75–'76; related, also, a few interesting anecdotes, and especially called his attention to the peculiar providence that tied the hands of our enemies until the proper time was come.

My second chapter, being a catalogue of names, the reader, after he has satisfied his curiosity in running over the little interesting sketch of the life of old Colonel Cresap, may, if he pleases, leave all the rest to examine when he has leisure.

My third chapter is short, containing little more than a brief view of the juvenile days of Captain Cresap. It is, however, in some degree, the key to the whole work, because it leads us to the cause and motives that led Captain Cresap to the Ohio in the Spring of the year 1774.

My fourth chapter contains the body, nerves and sinews of my book. In this chapter we are led to view many and important facts connected with Dunmore's war.

In preceding pages the reader has a view into the precarious state of the western country, the hostile attitude of our affairs with the Indians, and the slender thread of a dubious peace.

The Earl of Dunmore is introduced as suspected of combining his own influence, with predisposing causes, not only to set the Virginians and Pennsylvanians by the ears, but by artful and indirect means provoking a war with the Indians.

Arguments are adduced to prove the first, and circumstances produced to beget strong suspicion of the latter; and to elucidate these two important points I have devoted several pages.

But especially as to the latter—*i. e.*, the cause we have to suspect Dunmore as being concerned in producing the Indian war of 1774—we mentioned, as the first item in our list of suspicious circumstances, a circular letter from Dr. Connoly, his sub-governor and confidential agent at Pittsburg, warning the inhabitants to be on their guard,* &c. This letter I have applied as it ought to be applied—namely: to the justification of Captain Cresap, and every other person that considered it the herald and proclamation of war; and also as implying suspicion that it was designed to accelerate and make certain what was at the time only squally and threatening.

This letter, with the confirmatory messages as related in the chapter I am now analyzing, brought up Captain Cresap from some distance down the Ohio river to Wheeling, and in

---

* I must regret that I cannot lay my hands on this letter, but I not only recollect it, but recollect its motive and contents. Nor does the truth of this letter and its effects rest on my testimony only; Dr. Wheeler says the same.

conjunction with other facts and circumstances laid the foundation—and was in fact the real cause—of all the subsequent proceedings of Captain Cresap with the Indians, which are given in detail as they occurred.

I have also led the reader with Major McDonald and his little army to Wappatomica, on the Muskingum, and to the end of that campaign; then presented him with a view of Colonel Lewis and his fine body of western Virginians encamped at the mouth of Big Kanawha, and the sanguinary battle at that place.* Also, with the northern wing of the army under Dunmore in person, their march to the Scioto, treaty with the Indians, and conclusion of the war.

But I have interwoven throughout the course of this narrative several circumstances implying suspicion that Dunmore and Connoly were often moving ostensibly one way and covertly another; and as an argument evincive and confirmatory of this fact, we are led to a view of them naked and without a covering in the concluding scene of the drama; nor need

---

* This battle was the most bloody ever fought with the Indians within the limits of Virginia. Its sanguinary nature made it long remembered among the borderers, and its history is given in a rude song, which is even heard to the present day among the mountain cabins of that region:

Let us mind the tenth day of October,
　Seventy-four, which caused woe;
The Indian savages they did cover
　The pleasant banks of the Ohio.

The battle, beginning in the morning,
　Throughout the day it lashed sore,
Till the evening shades were returning down
　Upon the banks of the Ohio.

Judgment precedes to execution,
　Let fame throughout all dangers go;
Our heroes fought with resolution,
　Upon the banks of the Ohio.

Seven score lay dead and wounded,
　Of champions that did face their foe;

By which the heathen were confounded,
　Upon the banks of the Ohio.

Colonel Lewis and some noble captains
　Did down to death like Uriah go,
Alas! their heads wound up in napkins,
　Upon the banks of the Ohio.

Kings lamented their mighty fallen
　Upon the mountains of Gilboa;
And now we mourn for brave Hugh Allen,
　Far from the banks of the Ohio.

O, bless the mighty King of Heaven
　For all his wondrous works below,
Who hath to us the victory given,
　Upon the banks of the Ohio.

—*Howe's Great West, p.* 82.

we thank them that it was not to the people of the West a most direful tragedy.

I have, in my fifth chapter, taken up, examined, exposed and refuted the famous Logan speech, and proved by the most respectable and indisputable testimony that it is a mere counterfeit; and even that counterfeit, base as it is, is still more base and detestable from the malignant interpolation foisted in, to serve no earthly purpose but to blacken the character of a most valuable and distinguished citizen.

O, ye philosophers, orators, poets and scribblers, how little, how contemptible do you feel, and should you feel! After bandying about from north to south, and from south to north again, this speech—after sporting with the name and fame of a man you never knew, and who, if alive, would chastise you as you deserve—how must you feel to be told, and have it proved in your teeth, that your Logan speech, your fine specimen of Indian oratory, is a lie, a counterfeit, and never in fact had any existence as a real Indian speech! No doubt Colonel Gibson, if alive, must be highly delighted with the compliment you pay him, and truly diverted at your credulity. But bark on, gentlemen; we know that fiests may with impunity bark at a dead lion.

My sixth chapter is devoted to an indispensable but very unpleasant subject; and I cannot but express my regret that truth and justice compel me to handle rather roughly a man I always esteemed. Dr. Doddridge, for some cause to me inexplicable, has thought proper, in a book he has lately published, to introduce the name and fame of my friend Captain Cresap, who has now been dead something more than fifty years, and to load his memory with many atrocious and scandalous crimes; and knowing, as I do from personal knowledge, that every item in his long list worth notice is either not true, or if true, so distorted, misrepresented and falsified in their coloring as to be actually untrue, I have therefore, as the most conspicuous as well as most compendious method, dissected and analyzed his various charges, and I trust satisfied a candid public that, Dr. Doddridge and his book to the contrary notwithstanding, Captain Cresap is entirely innocent of every charge against him. For shame, Doctor! You know the good book says—"Thou shalt not bear false witness against thy neighbor;" but this witness of yours is the more malignant and permanent in its kind, as you have embodied it in your book, with a view to send it down to all succeeding generations.

My seventh chapter concludes the short, eventful and active life of Captain Cresap. After marching a company of riflemen to Boston he is taken sick in camp, gets worse, sets off for home and reaches New York, where he dies, and is buried with military honors.

And here I advance an argument which I conceive conclusive and incontrovertible: that the very circumstance of his appointment to the command of this company is the strongest possible evidence of the high estimation in which he stood with his fellow citizens at that period, to-wit: in June, 1775; and that, as he died in less than four months after this date, and as his ashes have been honored and permitted to repose in peace for many years, is it not strange, and one of those mysteries that reason searches in vain for a cause, why they should be disturbed at this late period?

May I not be permitted to say that no benevolent heart, no heart in which is one drop of the milk of human kindness, that has either father or mother, brother or sister, wife or children, could or would, we should naturally suppose, merely for the sake of defamation, even admitting they had truth on their side, wish to wound the feelings of honorable and surviving relatives, merely to pour contempt and contumely upon the ashes of the dead. But how much worse, how much stronger the case when the devoted victim is an honest man!

And here I close my book, bidding adieu, I expect forever, at least in this world, to all Captain Cresap's accusers, calumniators and enemies, and pray God to forgive them; and that no unhallowed hands or tongues may disturb their ashes, some ten, or twenty, or fifty years after they are dead.

APPENDIX.

The first witness we introduce is Benjamin Tomlinson, Esq., who is still living—a man universally respected, and whose testimony no man dare to call in question. It is given by way of interrogatory.

Question 1st. What number of Indians were killed at Yellow Creek?

Answer. Logan's mother, younger brother, and sister, who was called Gibson's squaw; this woman had a child half white, which was not killed.

Ques. 2d. Do you recollect the time and circumstances of the affair at Yellow Creek?

Ans. Yes; the time was the third or fourth day of May, 1774, and the circumstances were that two or three days before these Indians were killed at Yellow Creek [the reader has not forgotten that this is precisely what I say in my fourth chapter, and the more gratifying to me as I had not Mr. Tomlinson's certificate then before me,] by the whites, two men were killed and one wounded in a canoe belonging to a Mr. Butler, of Pittsburg, as they were descending the Ohio river near the mouth of Little Beaver, [Little Beaver and Yellow Creek are not far apart,] and this canoe was plundered of all the property; and moreover, about this time the Indians were threatening the inhabitants about the river Ohio, [this I state in my fourth chapter also, and confirm it by Connoly's letter or proclamation,] and I was also informed they had committed some depredations on the property of Michael Cresap. I assisted in the burial of the white men killed in Butler's canoe.

Ques. 3d. Who commanded the party that killed the Indians at Yellow Creek, and who killed those Indians? Do you know?

Ans. The party had no commander. I believe Logan's brother was killed by a man named Sappington; who killed the others I do not know, although I was present. But this I well know—that neither Captain Michael Cresap nor any other person of that name was there, nor do I believe within many miles of the place.

Ques. 4th. Where was Logan's residence, and what was his character?

Ans. I believe his residence was on Muskingum. His character was no ways particular; he was only a common man among the Indians—no chief, no captain.

Ques. 5th. Where and when did Logan die?

Ans. To this question I answer, that I do not know when or where Logan died,* but was informed by Esquire Barkley, of Bedford, that he became very vile; that he killed his own wife, and was himself killed by her brother. I am, however, certain he did not die until after Dunmore's treaty on the Scioto.

---

* Logan, at an Indian Council held at Detroit, became wildly drunk, and, in the midst of delirious passion, prostrated his wife by a sudden blow. She fell before him apparently dead. In a moment, the horrid deed partly sobered the savage, who, thinking he had killed her, fled precipitately lest the stern Indian penalty of blood for blood might befall him at the hand of some relative of the murdered woman. While traveling alone, and still confused by liquor and the fear of vengeance, he was suddenly overtaken in the wilderness between Detroit and Sandusky, by a troop of Indians with their squaws and children, in the midst of whom he recognized his nephew or cousin Tod-kah-dohs. Bewildered as he was, he imagined that the lawful avenger pursued him in the form of his relative,—for the Indian rule permits a relation to perform the retributive act of revenge for murder,—and rashly bursting forth in frantic passion, he exclaimed that the whole party should fall beneath his weapons. Tod-kah-dohs, seeing their danger, and observing that Logan was well armed, told his companions that their only safety was in getting the advantage of the desperate man by prompt action. But Logan was quite as alert as his adversary; yet while leaping from his horse to execute his dreadful

Ques. 6th. Was Logan at the treaty held by Dunmore with the Indians at Camp Charlotte, on the Scioto? Did he make a speech? And if not, who made a speech for him?

Ans. To this question I answer: Logan was not at the treaty; perhaps Cornstalk, the chief of the Shawanee nation, mentioned among other grievances the Indians killed on Yellow Creek; but I believe neither Cresap nor any other persons were named as the perpetrators. I perfectly recollect that I was that day officer of the guard, and stood near Dunmore's person, and consequently I saw and heard all that passed; that also two or three days before the treaty, when I was on the out-guard, Simon Girty, who was passing by, stopped with me and conversed; he said he was going after Logan, but he did not like his business, for he was a surly fellow; he, however, proceeded on, and I saw him return on the day of the treaty, and Logan was not with him. At this time a circle was formed and the treaty begun. I saw John Gibson, on Girty's arrival, get up and go out of the circle and talk with Girty; after which he (Gibson) went into a tent, and soon after returning into the circle, drew out of his pocket a piece of clean, new paper, on which was written, in his own hand-writing, a speech for and in the name of Logan. This I heard read three times—once by Gibson and twice by Dun-

---

threat, Tod-kah-dohs leveled a shot-gun within a few feet of the savage and killed him on the spot!

Tod-kah-dohs, or The Searcher, originally from Conestoga, and *probably* a son of Logan's sister residing there, died, about 1844, at the cold spring on the Allegheny Seneca Reservation, nearly 100 years old. He was better known as Captain Logan, and was either a *nephew* or *cousin* of the celebrated Indian. He left children, two of whom have been seen by Mr. Draper; so that, in spite of Logan's speech, *some* of his "blood" *still* "*runs*" in human veins, 77 years after the Yellow Creek tragedy. The substance of this narrative was given me in MS. by Mr. Lyman C. Draper, who received it from Dah-gan-on-do, or Captain Decker, as it was related to him by Tod-kah-dohs, who killed Logan. "Decker," says Mr. Draper, "was a venerable Seneca Indian, and the best Indian chronicler I have met with. His narratives are generally sustained by other evidence, and never seem confused or improbable." Logan's wife, who was a Shawanese, and had no children by him, did not die in consequence of her husband's blow, but recovered and returned to her people.—*Brantz Mayer's Address, p.* 67.

12

more—the purport of which was, that he (Logan) was the white man's friend; that on a journey to Pittsburg to brighten this friendship, or on his return from thence, all his friends were killed at Yellow Creek; that now, when he died, who should bury him?—for the blood of Logan was running in no creature's veins; but neither was the name of Cresap or the name of any other person mentioned in this speech. But I recollect having seen Dunmore put this speech among the other treaty papers.

Ques. 7th. If Logan was not at the treaty, and made no speech, pray from whence came and who was the author of that famous speech?

Ans. In addition to what is stated above, I say there is no doubt in my mind that it originated altogether with and was framed and produced by Colonel John Gibson.

Ques. 8th. Do you recollect the names of any gentlemen who were present at the treaty?

Ans. Yes; I recollect the following persons, and believe they are still alive* and live at the following places, to-wit: General Daniel Morgan, Berkley county, Virginia; Colonel James Wood, now Governor of Virginia; Captain David Scott, Monongahela; Captain John Wilson, Kentucky; Lieutenant Gabriel Cox, Kentucky; Captain Johnson, Youghiogheny; Captain James Parsons, Moorfield; General George R. Clark, Captain William Harrod, Colonel L. Barret, Lieutenant Joseph Cresap and Captain Wm. Henshaw, Berkley.

[I believe most of these gentlemen are now (1826) dead.]

Ques. 9th. Was the question as to the origin of the war discussed at the treaty?

Ans. Yes; the Indians gave as a reason, the Indians killed at Yellow Creek, Whetstone Creek, Beech Bottom and else-

* This was on the 17th of April, 1797.

where. But the Indians were in fact the first aggressors, and committed the first hostilities.

Ques. 10*th.* Were not some white men killed by the Indians in the year 1773?

Ans. Yes; John Martin and two of his men were killed on Hockhocking, about one year before Dunmore's army went out, and his canoe was plundered of above £200 worth of goods.

I lived on the river Ohio, and near the mouth of Yellow Creek, from the year 1770 until the Indians were killed at Yellow Creek, and several years after; I was present when the Indians were killed, and also present at the treaty in September or October, 1774, near Chillicothe, on the Scioto; and certify that the foregoing statements of facts are true, to the best of my recollection.

[Signed] BENJAMIN TOMLINSON.
Cumberland, April 17, 1797.

We now present the reader with the testimony of Dr. Wheeler, a man equally respectable, but now dead. It is also in the same way of question and answer:

Question 1*st.* Do you know, or recollect to have heard, of the murder of John Martin and other Indian traders, on the Hockhocking, in 1773?

Answer. I recollect that John Martin and Guy Meeks were killed by the Indians in 1773; the former I personally knew, the latter I was acquainted with, but thought they had been killed at the mouth of Capteening.

Ques. 2*d.* Do you know, or have you heard, of two men that were killed and one that was wounded in a trading canoe belonging to Mr. Butler, of Pittsburg, at or near the mouth of Little Beaver, by the Indians? And did you hear that the canoe was plundered?

Ans. I heard an acquaintance say he was well acquainted with one of the men that was wounded in Butler's canoe, but whether it was plundered or not I cannot say.

The third question, not being answered, is omitted.

Ques. 4th. Was there not a bustle before or about the time Butler's men were killed—an express sent by Major Connoly,* the commandant at Pittsburg, warning the inhabitants to be on their guard, that the Indians were about to strike? And had not this express a written message, or circular letter?

Ans. There was a circular letter sent to the inhabitants of Redstone Old Fort by Major Connoly, for the purpose of warning them to be on their guard; but whether before or after Butler's canoe was robbed, I cannot tell.

Ques. 5th. Were there not about this time, to-wit: a little before any Indians were killed, a general panic and uneasy apprehensions among the people on the Ohio and its vicinity, fearing daily a stroke from the Indians? And were not the people flying in all directions to forts, &c?

Ans. To this question I can answer from experience, [the Doctor lived at this time about four or five miles west of the Monongahela,] and assert that it was the case.

Ques. 6th. Do you apprehend that when Captain Cresap went down the Ohio, in 1774, it was to fight Indians or improve lands?

---

* Dr. John Connoly, who played so prominent a part as commandant of Pittsburg, where he continued at least through 1774, was, from the outset of the Revolutionary movements, a tory; and being a man extensively acquainted with the West, a man of talent, and fearless withal, he naturally became a leader. This man, in 1775, planned a union of the north-western Indians with British troops, which combined forces were to be led, under his command, from Detroit, and, after ravaging the few frontier settlements, were to join Lord Dunmore in eastern Virginia. To forward his plans, Connoly visited Boston to see General Gage; then, having returned to the South, in the fall of 1775, he left Lord Dunmore for the West, bearing one set of instructions upon his person, and another set—the true ones—most artfully concealed under the direction of Lord Dunmore himself, in his saddle, secured by tin and waxed cloth. He and his comrades, among whom was Dr. Smyth, had gone as far as Hagerstown, where they were arrested upon suspicion and sent back to Frederick. There they were searched, and the papers upon Connoly's person were found, seized and sent to Con-

Ans. I can in justice say it was to improve lands.

Ques. 7th. Was Captain Cresap, or any of the Cresaps, at Yellow Creek when the Indians were killed at that place, and where was he?

Ans. At the time the Indians were killed on Yellow Creek Captain Cresap was at Wheeling. *Greathouse* killed Logan's sister at Yellow Creek.

Ques. 8th. Do you apprehend that if Captain Cresap had not heard of Connoly's message, of the murder committed in Butler's canoe, nor seen nor heard of anything hostile in the Indians, that he would ever have attacked them?

Ans. It was evident Captain Cresap was much interested at that time in improving lands for himself; therefore it can not in reason be thought he would, to his injury, have encouraged an Indian war, to the hindrance of that business and to his loss; but, being well assured of the hostile disposition of the Indians, he, like a man of spirit and resolution, armed himself and others against their attacks.

Ques. 9th. [Omitted, as it is implied and answered above.]

Ques. 10th. Was Captain Cresap a man infamous for his many Indian murders? When, where, and who were the Indians killed by him before the year 1774?

Ans. I was closely acquainted with Captain Cresap at the time he was over the Monongahela river, and with truth

---

gress. Washington having been informed by one who was present when the genuine instructions were concealed as above stated, wrote twice on the subject to the proper authorities, in order to lead to their discovery, but we do not learn that they were ever found. Connoly himself was confined, and remained a close prisoner till 1781, complaining much of his hard lot, but finding few to pity him.

Connoly, soon after, was for a short time released by the sheriff, upon the promise to return to the law's custody, which promise he broke, however, and having collected a band of followers, on the 28th of March, came again to Pittsburg, still asserting the claim of Virginia to the government. Then commenced a series of contests, outrages and complaints, which were too extensive and complicated to be described within our limited space. The upshot of the matter was this, that Connoly, in Lord Dunmore's name, and by his authority, took and kept possession of Fort Pitt; and as it had been dismantled and nearly destroyed, by royal orders, rebuilt it, and named it Fort Dunmore.—*Perkins's Annals of the West, pp.* 151, 122.

assert that he killed no Indian before the year 1774. But a little before McDonald's campaign, Captain Cresap went on a scout with a few men to the frontier, at which time he killed and scalped an Indian man; he had also a man named Masterson wounded in the groin in the engagement.

Ques. 11th. If Captain Cresap had no reason to apprehend an attack from the Indians, why did he leave his lands and business and ascend the Ohio twenty or thirty miles to the nearest place of safety—*i. e.*, Wheeling—when he had at the same time eight or ten men hired at $6 50 per month, and their loss of time must have been to him a serious injury? Say what you think and believe of this.

Ans. Captain Cresap frequented my house, *alias* cabin, on his way out and return from the frontier, and I remember his observing the great disappointment and injury he had sustained from the hostile disposition of the Indians at that time, as it prevented his improving the lands he had taken up.

Ques. 12th. How do Indians begin their war—with proclamations or with scalping-knives?

Ans. It has been unhappily experienced that Indians have no honor or regular form with white inhabitants; before going to war their first proclamation is gun, tomahawk and knife.

With respect to this certificate of Dr. Wheeler, it is proper to remark that the interrogatories were sent to him in a letter; that he himself set down the answers, and sent them back, also in a letter; so that what he says is entirely his own, neither myself nor any other friend of Captain Cresap being present; and this accounts for the defect as to date—his envelope being mislaid.

We now, thirdly, add the testimony of General Minor:

"I do hereby certify that I was intimately and particularly

"acquainted with the late Captain Michael Cresap, as well
"before as after the Indian war of 1774, called Dunmore's
"war; that from that intimacy I not only believe but am well
"assured that the object of his journey to the Ohio in the
"Spring of the year 1774 was not to fight Indians; that after
"the rencounter or skirmish that took place between Captain
"Cresap and some Indians on the Ohio, near Grave Creek,
[this is Dr. Doddridge's Capteening battle, and Dr. Wheeler
alludes to the same battle when he says Captain Cresap killed
an Indian man and had one man wounded,] "I was frequently
"in his company, and always when the subject of that fight
"was introduced, heard him say that no man dared to charge
"him with making an unjust or improper attack upon Indians;
"and that while he, the said Cresap, was on the Ohio, he re-
"ceived a message from Major Connoly, commandant at Pitts-
"burg, Mr. Alexander McKee, and I believe Colonel Croghan,
"giving him (Cresap) notice that he must be on his guard—
"that the Indians were about to strike, and manifested a very
"hostile disposition.

"I further certify that from my long and intimate acquaint-
"ance with Captain Cresap, I believe and am certain that he
"ought not, nor could not with justice and propriety, be
"deemed a man infamous for murdering Indians, nor in any
"other point of view. He was, it is true, a good soldier, and
"report says (which I believe) that he shot an Indian with a
"pistol while he (the Indian) was attempting to scalp a Mr.
"Welder that the Indian had killed at Old Town many years
"before Dunmore's war, and while Cresap was a youth.

"Given under my hand this 24th September, 1800.
    [Signed]   "JOHN MINOR, *B. G. of Militia.*"
    "*Witness:* Evan Gwynn, Justice of the Peace for Alle-
"gheny county."

To which certificate General Minor adds, that he recollects having heard Captain Cresap speak with pointed disapprobation of the Indian massacre at Yellow Creek.

I have all these original certificates by me, which any skeptical reader is at liberty to consult.

But now to conclude the whole, if I may be permitted to add my own testimony, I say that from my intimate personal acquaintance with Captain Cresap and the most minute circumstance in his public life, all of which I have faithfully detailed in the preceding memoir, I am absolutely certain that he had no more concern, either directly or indirectly, in the murder of Logan's relations, than he had in stabbing Julius Cæsar, or cutting off Pompey's head; and that there is no more reason to stigmatize him as a detestable Indian murderer, than Hancock, Adams, Washington and Jefferson as rebels and traitors; neither is there any more justice in saddling him with all the carnage, blood and awful consequences of Dunmore's war, than to charge Dr. Doddridge with setting fire to the theater in Richmond and burning the Governor of Virginia.

I have, however, in reserve an anecdote, which indeed at this late period may be considered rather a work of supererogation, yet as it is directly in point as to the Logan speech, and has not yet been told, I think it best the reader should have it:

Some ten or twelve years ago, in a little journey I took to the West, I called and tarried a day at Wheeling, and lodged with my old friend Colonel Zane. After dinner we took a walk into town, and stepped into a tavern, where several gentlemen were just finishing their dinners. We sat down, and the conversation soon turned upon Mr. Jefferson's Notes, when a gentleman from New York—of the name, if I recollect right, of Miller—said he must continue to think that what Mr. Jefferson had said respecting Cresap's* killing Logan's family, was certainly true.

I replied: "Sir, I thought Mr. Martin had put that question to rest."

He said: "No, sir; I have seen Mr. Martin's piece, and he has not satisfied my mind."

I then said: "If so, sir, I am happy to have it in my power to satisfy you upon the spot."

He seemed pleased with this, and observed that he should be glad to get at the truth. I then addressed myself to Col. Zane, and said:

"I think, Colonel, you know something about this business?"

He replied: "Yes, I do. I was here at Wheeling at the time Logan's relations were killed on Yellow Creek, and Captain Cresap was here also with me."

I then addressed Colonel Chaplaine, and said: "It is probable you also know something of this business, Colonel?"

He replied: "Yes, I know very well, for I was here, and know that Captain Cresap was also here."

I then turned to Mr. Miller and said: "Are you now satisfied, sir?"

He replied: "Yes; and gratified and glad to get at the real truth." I think I then requested him, upon all proper occasions, to state the fact as he now knew it, which I believe he promised to do.

---

* Gibson, it is true, states in his testimony that he corrected Logan on the spot when he made the charge against Cresap, for he knew his innocence, but either the Indian did not withdraw it or the messenger felt himself compelled to deliver it as originally framed. When it was read in camp, the pioneer soldiers knew it to be false as to Michael Cresap; but it only produced a laugh in the crowd, which displeased the Maryland Captain. *George Rogers Clark,* who was near, exclaimed, that "he must be a very great man, as the Indians palmed every thing that happened on his shoulders!" The Captain smiled and replied that "he had a **great** inclination to tomahawk Greathouse for the murder!"—*Brantz Mayer's Address, p.* 61.

If, then, truth is not falsehood and facts are not lies, it must be evident from the plain and incontrovertible statement I have laid before the public of the life of Captain Cresap, that none of the many malicious and reiterated charges against him have any foundation in fact. I can, therefore, and do, confidently appeal to the world, and ask, in the name of candor, justice, mercy and truth, to what particular period, to what circumstance, to what public or private act in the life of Captain Cresap can we point our finger and say—"Here is the murderer of Logan's family;" or, "here is the infamous murderer of Indians;" or, "here is the man that was the primary and first moving cause of Dunmore's war, or in any way the cause of that war."

F I N I S.

If there is any error in the foregoing narrative it is in the chronology. The author has lost or mislaid some important papers, and consequently has in some instances supplied the defect from memory, but thinks he is even substantially correct in this also — and especially as in one instance he has tested his accuracy by a record.

SUPPLEMENT.

As the author of the foregoing sketch had nothing in view but to rescue from public odium and infamy the name and character of a friend, he therefore turned his attention wholly and only to some remarks made by Mr. Jefferson in his celebrated Notes on Virginia, and to Dr. Doddridge's chapter on Dunmore's war. The residue of the Doctor's book escaped his notice and attention until his manuscript went to the press. But, being now relieved from that intense application indispensable in the prosecution of his work, and other multifarious concerns, he has leisurely and attentively traveled through the Doctor's book, and must say he is sorry to find so many things in that book that merit animadversion.

On page 101, the Doctor says that *"those atrocious murders of the peaceable and inoffensive Indians at Capteening and Yellow Creek, brought on the war of Lord Dunmore in the Spring of the year 1774."* Very good; but he forgets to tell us that, two or three days before this atrocious murder at Yellow Creek, and several days before his assumed fact of the atrocious murder at Capteening, these Indians, or some other Indians, (to retort his own language) were guilty of the atrocious murder of two or three men in Mr. Butler's canoe, near the mouth of Little Beaver, almost in the neighborhood of Yellow Creek, and no doubt was the cause of that strong excitement and irritation that eventuated in the massacre at that place.

But let us hear what the Doctor says himself respecting

these "peaceable and inoffensive Indians." Page 117 he tells us that "*the Indian mode of warfare was an indiscriminate slaughter of all ages and both sexes.*" Again, page 125—but marked in his book 132—he says his "*uncle Teter's hunting-camp was so judiciously and artfully selected, that, unless by the report of his gun or the sound of his ax, it would have been by mere accident if an Indian had discovered his concealment.*" So, then, it seems his uncle was a little suspicious of these peaceable fellows. And if the Doctor is correct in what he immediately adds, his uncle certainly acted wisely; for on the same page he (the Doctor) says, "*the hunters were often surprised and killed in their camps.*"

But that the reader may more clearly see what peaceable fellows these Indians are, or then were, we will present him with a few more extracts from the Doctor's book. Page 133, under the title of "The Wedding," in portraying the simplicity and rustic manners of that period, he says, among other things, that "it was a custom for some of the company to take Black Betty—*i. e.*, the whisky bottle—in their hands and say, 'Here's health to the groom, not forgetting myself; and here's to the bride—thumping luck and big children.' This, so far from being taken amiss, was considered an expression of a very proper and friendly wish; for big children, especially sons, were of great importance, as we were few in number, and engaged in perpetual hostility with the Indians, the end of which no one could foresee."

Again, on page 139, he says that "the early settlers on the frontiers of this country were like Arabs of the deserts of Africa, at least in two respects: Every man was a soldier, and from early in the Spring till late in the Fall was almost continually in arms. Their work was carried on by parties, each of whom had his rifle and everything belonging to his war dress. These were deposited in some central place in the field, a sentinel was stationed on the outside of the fence, so that on the least alarm the whole company repaired to their arms, and were ready for the combat in a moment."

Now, from my own knowledge of the state of things in the western country at the period alluded to by the Doctor, I can add my testimony that the statement he has made is tolerably correct; yet candor compels me to say that the shades he has drawn are rather too dark, because it is not exactly true that the first settlers were engaged in perpetual hostility; if so, Dunmore's war of 1774 could have had no origin,* and must have been nothing more than a continuation of pre-existing hostility, and could be in no other way distinguishable from the preceding time than by the increase of forces on each side, and the fury of the combatants; and the fact, I believe, is, that there were some short periods of precarious peace, or suspension of hostilities, although the people never thought themselves secure from attacks from the savages.

But, admitting the dark picture the Doctor has given us of the savage nature and conduct of the Indians to be correct, I ask, what are we to do with his bright side? He calls them a *"peaceable and inoffensive"* people, and proves it by declaring that their "mode of warfare was an indiscriminate slaughter of all ages and both sexes;" that they frequently killed the hunters in their camps, and that they were engaged in perpetual hostility with the early settlers on the frontier. Now, if this is the character of "peaceable and in-offensive" people, I, for one, would beg to be excused from residing in their neighborhood.

But it seems when the Doctor is disposed to abuse white people—Captain Cresap especially—he lays a white ground

* Page 225, the Doctor says the western settlers had peace from 1764 to 1774.

13

for his profile in the character of the Indians, that the reader may trace more accurately the black lines of his picture.* And *vice versa*—when he wishes to puff and trumpet the fame and delineate the sufferings of the early settlers on the frontiers, why then, to be sure, the Indians are dreadful fellows— ferocious savages, murdering indiscriminately old and young, male and female, killing the hunters in their camps, and granting the people no respite, no peace, but war, war, unceasing hostility.

But, I thank God that however just and accurate the Doctor's pencil may be in delineating those gloomy days of wars and blood, I trust the scene has changed, and is rapidly changing, into circumstances vastly more congenial to the feelings and wishes of all who love peace, and whose bosoms swell with an ardent and pure desire to see our Aceldama— our world of blood—changed, revolutionized, and converted into a world of peace and love, of harmony and universal good will among men; and that the time is come, or near at hand, when the savage yell and war-whoop of an Indian shall no more be heard—to the terror of the helpless female and feeble infant—echoing through our hills; but on the contrary, white men, red men and black men shall sweetly unite in harmonious anthems of praise and loud hallelujahs to God and the Lamb; when our American wilderness and solitary places shall be glad, and our desert, as far as the Pacific ocean, shall blossom as the rose.

But to return to the Doctor. I think it probable he will attempt to escape from the nook into which he has so unguardedly wedged himself, in some way or other. But we will save him the trouble by anticipating and examining every hole and

---

* Others that are really guilty, and certainly deserve the severest censure—as, for instance, the murderers of Old Cornstalk and his son and the Moravian Indians—he just brushes with a feather.

path through which he may attempt to escape. In the first place, if he says the description he has given us of the ferocious and savage nature of Indians has no reference to a period antecedent to Dunmore's war, we meet him with his own words. He tells us that the settlement between the Monongahela and the Laurel Ridge commenced in the year 1772, and that in the succeeding year they reached as far as the Ohio river. [I think, however, it was one year sooner.] But be this as it may, these settlements were anterior to Dunmore's war; and that he refers to the period of the first settlement of the country he tells us himself, for he says the *early settlers* were in a state of perpetual hostility or almost always at war with the Indians.

But only let us suppose that his meaning is, that those Indians who were killed at Yellow Creek and Capteening were "peaceable and inoffensive." Now, supposing this to be his meaning, we answer, that although these Indians at this particular period at Yellow Creek might have had no hostile intentions, yet it is absolutely certain, as I have already remarked, that only a day or two before this affair these Indians, or some of this party, or some other Indians, had killed two or three white men in Butler's canoe, near Yellow Creek ; and moreover, that Captain Cresap, on whom the Doctor seems anxious to throw the whole weight of Dunmore's war, had no more concern in that business than Dr. Doddridge himself; nor was he by many miles as near the scene of action as his reverence.

Again, that Cresap may by no means escape the bitterness of the Doctor's pen, he has coupled—unfairly, unjustly, and, I may add, contrary to all rules of propriety and candor in a historian—two things different in their nature, and at a distance as to time, place and circumstances. The atrocious murder, he says, of the peaceable, inoffensive Indians at Yellow Creek and Capteening, brought on the war of Lord Dunmore, in the Spring of the year 1774. Now, as I have already set this affair at Capteening before the reader in the clearest light, and proved that, so far from being an atrocious murder, it was a regular battle, in which both parties were engaged, and one man at least killed or wounded on each side, and that it was several days after the affair at Yellow Creek, and many miles distant from it, hence I suppose it is needless to add anything here to repel this deadly blow aimed at the fair fame of Captain Cresap.

But, as our extreme anxiety to rescue from unmerited odium the character of a deceased friend, has led us to handle the Doctor a little roughly, we will with great pleasure eke out for him the best apology we can devise, or that presents itself to our view, and this, too, from himself—to-wit: In the second page of his address to his readers, he says that the history of our Indian wars (his own history) is in every respect quite imperfect, and that the very limited range of the war he had in view in this work is not fully accomplished; and on his next page he adds that the whole amount of his present memorials of this widely-extended warfare consists of merely detached narratives, and these for the most part badly written, in many instances destitute of historical precision (and no doubt chronological also). And in the second page of his preface he holds the same language, and says the want of printed documents was not the only difficulty he had to contend with; that when he traveled beyond the bounds of his own memory (which I presume was no great journey) he found it extremely difficult to procure information from the living which he wished to relate.

Now, I suppose, if language has any meaning, the natural

inference from all this is, that the Doctor had at best but an imperfect, partial and superficial acquaintance with the facts, or assumed facts stated in his history; and therefore, without any reflection upon his veracity as a historian, we may presume he has been led into numberless errors, mistakes, and even contradictions, from the incorrect, partial and mutilated testimony of incompetent and ignorant witnesses; and if so, his errors are rather to be attributed to improper credulity than malevolence, and to negligence in not cautiously collating and examining his materials. But we must be permitted to remark, however, that after admitting the foregoing as some apology for errors and mistakes in a historian, yet it does not follow that any man is justifiable in recording as facts, and handing them down to posterity as such, any matters or things doubtful in their nature and uncertain as to their truth in his own mind; and more especially when those doubtful facts and circumstances have a direct tendency to consign to perpetual infamy the character of a respectable fellow citizen.

As to any recollection the Doctor himself could pretend to have as to any matter or thing beyond the bounds of his father's cornfield at the period he so emphatically alludes to— to-wit: 1772-'73-'74—it must certainly be very limited and imperfect, for he was then very young. Therefore, when his own knowledge with all its strength is combined with the information he received from others as to the truth and certainty of the facts he records, it will only amount at last to mere conjecture, which the reader is at liberty to think of as he pleases. And as it was impossible that any man could write a correct history from the materials in the Doctor's hands, he has therefore only left undone what no man could possibly do.

June 5, 1826.

CONCLUSION.

In bidding adieu to my opponents, I would take the liberty to observe that I am at peace with them and all mankind, and therefore extremely regret that what I conceived to be indispensable duty, and indeed imperious necessity, over which an accordance with my feelings I scarcely can say I had control, I have been urged and propelled to launch into a field quite new to me, discordant to my wishes, and in good degree at variance with my habits and the general course of my pursuits. If, therefore, in pursuing with a steady eye the main object I had in view—namely: rescuing from undeserved infamy the character of a friend and the reputation of a respectable family, identified inevitably and involved unavoidably in the attempted stigma upon the character of one of the most brilliant and conspicuous characters of the name—if, I say, in pursuing this object necessity has compelled me to name some very respectable gentlemen, I hope those gentlemen and all the world will see that it was impossible to avoid it; for I can and do assure those gentlemen that if any method could possibly have been thought of or devised to defend the character of Captain Cresap and at the same time cover them with the mantle of love, it should have been done; but as this was not possible, I must therefore entreat those gentlemen to accept as an apology for any tart expressions or apparent unfriendly remarks they may discover in my work, my extreme anxiety to obliterate from the minds of my fellow citizens those prejudices, and premature, prejudged and erroneous opinions they must, from what they have seen and heard, have imbibed respecting the character of the man I defend. More especially, the venerable age of our honorable ex-President certainly merits respect; and I can and do assure that gentleman that it would be more congenial with my feelings to offer him a cordial, or something to exhilarate, rather than depress the spirit or wound the feelings of an old man, with whom my own feelings, even in the absence of better motives, would teach me to sympathize.

Finally, as it is possible that under a momentary impulse I may have been led beyond the bounds of cool and dispassionate argument, if so, I beg those gentlemen's pardon, and hope they will attribute it to the right motive—namely: an ardent wish to do the same thing that they themselves, if placed in my circumstances, would certainly have done, *i. e.*, to rescue from infamy the character of a highly esteemed friend. May you, gentlemen, notwithstanding all you have said and written against Captain Cresap, and all I have written in refutation of those charges, enjoy felicity and happiness in the present world, and unceasing pleasure and joy unspeakable in the world to come.

THE AUTHOR.

June 5, 1826.

The author thinks it proper to inform the public, and especially the friends of Dr. Doddridge, that, notwithstanding the unjust attack of the Doctor upon the character of his deceased friend Captain Cresap, and his determination to refute those charges, yet, being anxious to treat him personally with all possible candor, he addressed to him a letter, written as early as May last, but was utterly at a loss where to direct the letter (as he understood the Doctor had removed to the State of Ohio, and he knew not to what place); consequently the letter was never sent; and as the Doctor is now dead, the opportunity is lost of giving him any notice of his intention.

GENERAL CLARK'S ACCOUNT.

[The publisher deems it proper to introduce here, as bearing directly upon the subject matter of this book, the following letter from General George Rogers Clark, in vindication of Captain Cresap. It was addressed to Samuel Brown, Esq., and dated June 17, 1798.]

The conduct of Cresap I am perfectly acquainted with. He was not the author of that murder, [of Logan's family,] but a family by the name of Greathouse.

This country was explored in 1773. A resolution was formed to make a settlement the Spring following, and the mouth of the Little Kanawha appointed the place of general rendezvous, in order to descend the river from there in a body. Early in the Spring the Indians had done some mischief. Reports from their towns were alarming, which deterred many. About eighty or ninety men only met at the appointed rendezvous, where we lay some days.

A small party of hunters that lay about ten miles below us were fired upon by the Indians, whom the hunters beat back, and returned to camp. This and many other circumstances led us to believe that the Indians were determined on war. The whole party was enrolled, and determined to execute their project of forming a settlement in Kentucky, as we had every necessary store that could be thought of. An Indian town called the Horsehead Bottom, on the Scioto and near its mouth, lay nearly in our way. The determination was to cross the country and surprise it. Who was to command? was the question. There were but few among us that had experience in Indian warfare, and they were such that we did not choose to be commanded by. We knew of Captain Cresap being on the river about fifteen miles above us, with some hands, settling a plantation, and that he had concluded to follow us to Kentucky as soon as he had fixed there his people. We also knew that he had been experienced in a former war. He was proposed, and it was unanimously agreed to send for him to command the party. Messengers were dispatched, and in half an hour returned with Cresap. He had heard of our resolution by some of his hunters that had fallen in with ours, and had set out to come to us.

We now thought our army, as we called it, complete, and the destruction of the Indians sure. A council was called, and to our astonishment our intended commander-in-chief was the person that dissuaded us from the enterprise. He said that appearances were very suspicious, but there was no certainty of a war; that if we made the attempt proposed he had no doubt of our success, but a war would at any rate be the result, and that we should be blamed for it, and perhaps justly; but if we were determined to proceed, he would lay aside all considerations, send to his camp for his people, and share our fortunes. He was then asked what he would advise. His answer was, that we should return to Wheeling, as a convenient post, to hear what was going forward; that a few weeks would determine; as it was early in the Spring, if we found the Indians were not disposed for war, we should have full time to return and make our establishment in Kentucky. This was adopted, and in two hours the whole were under way. As we ascended the river we met Killbuck, an Indian chief, with a small party. We had a long conference with him, but received little satisfaction as to the disposition of the Indians. It was observed that Cresap did not come to this conference, but kept on the opposite side of the river. He said that he was afraid to trust himself with the Indians; that Killbuck had frequently attempted to waylay his father, to kill him ; that if he crossed the river perhaps his fortitude might fail him, and that he might put Killbuck to death. On our arrival at Wheeling (the country being pretty well settled thereabouts) the whole of the inhabitants appeared to be alarmed. They flocked to our camp from every direction, and all that we could say could not keep them from under our wings. We offered to cover their neighborhood with our scouts until further information, if they would return to their plantations; but nothing would prevail. By this time we had got to be a formidable party. All the hunters, men without families, etc., in that quarter, had joined our party. Our arrival at Wheeling was soon known at Pittsburg. The whole of that country at that time being under the jurisdiction of Virginia, Dr. Connoly had been appointed by Dunmore Captain Commandant of the District, which was called West Augusta. He, learning of us, sent a message addressed to the party, letting us know that a war was to be apprehended, and requesting that we would keep our position for a few days, as messages had been sent to the Indians, and a few days would determine the doubt. The answer he got was, that we had no inclination to quit our quarters for some time; that during our stay we should be careful that the enemy should not harass the neighborhood that we lay in. But before this answer could reach Pittsburg he sent a second express, addressed to Captain Cresap, as the most influential man among us, informing him that the messages had returned from the

Indians, that war was inevitable, and begging him to use his influence with the party to get them to cover the country by scouts until the inhabitants could fortify themselves. The reception of this letter was the epoch of open hostilities with the Indians. A new post was planted, a council was called, and the letter read by Cresap—all the Indian traders being summoned on so important an occasion. Action was had, and war declared in the most solemn manner; and the same evening two scalps were brought into camp.

The next day some canoes of Indians were discovered on the river, keeping the advantage of an island to cover themselves from our view. They were chased fifteen miles down the river, and driven ashore. A battle ensued—a few were wounded on both sides—one Indian only taken prisoner. On examining their canoes we found a considerable quantity of ammunition and other warlike stores. On our return to camp a resolution was adopted to march the next day and attack Logan's camp on the Ohio, about thirty miles above us. We did march about five miles, and then halted to take some refreshment. Here the impropriety of executing the projected enterprise was argued. The conversation was brought forward by Cresap himself. It was generally agreed that those Indians had no hostile intentions, as they were hunting, and their party was composed of men, women and children, with all their stuff with them. This we knew, as I myself and others present had been in their camp about four weeks past, on our descending the river from Pittsburg. In short, every person seemed to detest the resolution we had set out with. We returned in the evening, decamped, and took the road to Redstone.

It was two days after this that Logan's family were killed. And from the manner in which it was done, it was viewed as a horrid murder. From Logan's hearing of Cresap being at the head of this party on the river, it is no wonder that he supposed he had a hand in the destruction of his family.

Since the reception of your letter I have procured the "Notes on Virginia." They are now before me. The act was more barbarous than there related by Mr. Jefferson. Those Indians used to visit and to return visits with the neighboring whites, on the opposite side of the river. They were on a visit to a family of the name of Greathouse, at the time they were murdered by them and their associates.

The war now raged in all its savage fury until the Fall, when a treaty of peace was held at Camp Charlotte, within four miles of Chillicothe, the Indian capital of the Ohio. Logan did not appear. I was acquainted with him, and wished to know the reason. The answer was, that he was like a mad dog; his bristles had been up, and were not yet quite fallen, but the good talk now going forward might allay them. Logan's speech to Dunmore now came forward, as related by Mr. Jefferson. It was thought to be clever, though the army knew it to be wrong as to Cresap; but it only produced a laugh in camp. I saw it displeased Captain Cresap, and told him that he must be a very great man—that the Indians palmed every thing that happened on his shoulders. He smiled and said that he had an inclination to tomahawk Greathouse for the murder.

What I have related is fact. I was intimate with Cresap. Logan I was better acquainted with, at that time, than with any other Indian in the western country. I was perfectly acquainted with the conduct of both parties. Logan was the author of the speech, as altered by Mr. Jefferson; and Cresap's conduct was as I have here related it.

A

JOURNAL

OF

WAYNE'S CAMPAIGN.

BEING AN AUTHENTIC DAILY RECORD OF THE MOST IMPORTANT OCCUR-
RENCES DURING THE CAMPAIGN OF MAJOR GENERAL
ANTHONY WAYNE, AGAINST THE

NORTHWESTERN INDIANS;

COMMENCING ON THE 28TH DAY OF JULY, AND ENDING ON THE 2D DAY
OF NOVEMBER, 1794; INCLUDING AN ACCOUNT OF THE
GREAT BATTLE OF AUGUST 20TH.

————◆————

BY LIEUTENANT BOYER.

————◆————

CINCINNATI, O.:
PRINTED FOR WILLIAM DODGE,
By JNO. F. UHLHORN.
1 8 6 6.

14

DAILY JOURNAL OF WAYNE'S CAMPAIGN,

From July 28th to November 2d, 1794, including an account of the memorable battle of 20th August.

Fort Greenville—where we were employed in erecting huts, and remained until the 28th July, 1794.

Camp at Stillwater, 28th July, 1794.—Agreeable to the general order of yesterday, the legion took up their line of march at 8 o'clock, and encamped at half past 3 on the bank of Stillwater, twelve miles from Greenville. The weather extremely warm—water very bad. Nothing occurred worth noticing.

Camp one mile in advance of Fort Recovery, 29th July, 1794. At 5 o'clock left the camp; arrived on this ground at 1 o'clock, being fifteen miles. Nothing took place worth reciting.

I am now informed that tracks were perceived on our right flank, supposed to be runners from the Oglaize.

Camp Beaver Swamp, eleven miles in advance of Fort Recovery, 30th July, 1794.—This morning the legion took up the line of march, and arrived here at 3 o'clock. The road was to cut, as will be the case on every new route we take in this country. The weather still warm—no water except in ponds, which nothing but excessive thirst would induce us to drink. The mosquitoes are very troublesome, and larger than I ever saw. The most of this country is covered with beech, the land of a wet soil intermixed with rich tracts, but no running water to be found. A bridge to be built over this swamp to-morrow, which prevents the march of the legion till the day after. We are informed there is no water for twelve miles.

July 31*st*, 1794.—Commenced building the bridge—being seventy yards in length—which will require infinite labor; it will be five feet deep, with loose mud and water.

One hundred pioneers set out this morning, strongly escorted, to cut a road to the St. Mary's river, twelve miles. I expect the bridge will be completed so as to march early in the morning.

Camp St. Mary's River, August 1*st*, 1794.—Proceeded on our way before sunrise, and arrived at this place at 3 o'clock, being twelve miles as aforesaid. Our encampment is on the largest and most beautiful prairie I ever beheld, the land rich and well timbered; the water plenty, but very bad; the river is from forty-five to fifty yards wide, in which I bathed. I am told there is plenty of fish in it.

August 2*d,* 1794.—The legion detained here for the purpose of erecting a garrison, which will take up three days. This day one of the deputy quartermasters was taken up by the Indians. Our spies discovered where four of the enemy had retreated precipitately with a horse, and supposed to be the party the above person had been taken by. It is hoped he will not give accurate information of our strength.

August 3*d*, 1794.—An accident took place this day by a tree falling on the commander-in-chief and nearly putting an end to his existence; we expected to be detained here some time in consequence of it, but fortunately he is not so much hurt as to prevent him from riding at a slow pace. No appearance of the enemy to-day, and think they are preparing for a warm attack. The weather very hot and dry, without any appearance of rain.

Camp thirty-one miles in advance of Fort Recovery, 4th August, 1794.— The aforesaid garrison being completed, Lieutenant Underhill, with one hundred men, left to protect it; departed at 6 o'clock and arrived here at 3 o'clock, being ten miles. The land we marched through is rich and well timbered, but the water scarce and bad; obliged to dig holes in boggy places and let it settle.

Camp forty-four miles in advance of Fort Recovery, 5th August, 1794.—We arrived at this place at 4 o'clock, nothing particular occurring. The land and water as above described—had some rain to-day.

Camp fifty-six miles from Fort Recovery, 6th August, 1794. Encamped on this ground at 2 o'clock. In the course of our march perceived the track of twenty Indians. I am informed we are within six miles of one of their towns on the Oglaize river, supposed to be the upper Delaware town. If so, I expect to eat green corn to-morrow. Our march this day has been through an exceeding fine country, but the water still bad; the day cooler than heretofore.

Camp sixty-eight miles from Fort Recovery, 7th August, 1794. This day passed the upper town on the Oglaize, which the Indians evacuated some time ago. I expect to see one of their new towns, where I am told there are all sorts of vegetables, which will be very acceptable to the troops. We have had no appearance of Indians to-day.

Camp Grand Oglaize, 8th August, 1794.—Proceeded on our march to this place at 5 o'clock this morning, and arrived here at the confluence of the Miami and Oglaize rivers at half past 10, being seventy-seven miles from Fort Recovery. This place far excels in beauty any in the western country, and believed equalled by none in the Atlantic States. Here are vegetables of every kind in abundance, and we have marched four or five miles in cornfields down the Oglaize, and there is not less than one thousand acres of corn round the town. The land in general of the fir nature. This country appears well adapted for the enjoyment of industrious people, who cannot avoid living in as great luxury as in any other place throughout the States, Nature having lent a most bountiful hand in the arrangement of the position, that a man can send the produce to market in his own boat. The land level and river navigable, not more than sixty miles from the lake. The British have built a large garrison about fifty miles from this place, and our spies inform us that the enemy are encamped about two miles above it, on the river.

Grand Oglaize, 9th August, 1794.— We remain here. The commander-in-chief has ordered a garrison to be erected at the confluence of the Miami and Oglaize rivers, which was begun this morning, and will take up some time; by this means the troops will be much refreshed, as well as the horses and cattle, the latter being much wearied and in need of a recess of labor. No appearance of an enemy.

Grand Oglaize, 10th August, 1794.— The troops in good spirits. No interruption from, or account of, the enemy. We have plenty of vegetables. One of our militia officers was wounded by his own sentinel by mistake.

Grand Oglaize, 11th August, 1794.—Nothing occurs to prevent the completion of our work.   *   *   *   *   *

Took up the line of march, and at 1 arrived on this ground without any occurrence. Our camp is situated in sight of Snaketown, on the Miami of the Lake. Vegetables in abundance.

Camp nineteen miles from Oglaize, 16th August, 1794.—Our march this day was through a bushy ground, and the road generally bad. Miller (the flag) returned this day from the enemy with information from the tribes, that if the commander-in-chief would remain at Grand Oglaize ten days they would let him know whether they would be for peace or war.

Camp thirty-one miles from Grand Oglaize, 17th August, 1794. This day a small party of the enemy's spies fell in with ours; both parties being for discoveries, they retreated, at which time the enemy fired and wounded one of our horses. Our camp, head of the Rapids.

Camp forty-one miles from Grand Oglaize, 18th August, 1794. The legion arrived on this ground, nothing particular taking place. Five of our spies were sent out at 3 o'clock—they fell in with an advanced body of the enemy, and obliged to retreat; but May, one of our spies, fell under the enemy's hold. What his fate may be must be left to future success.

Camp Deposit, 19th August, 1794.—The legion still continued in encampment, and are throwing up works to secure and deposit the heavy baggage of the troops, so that the men may be light for action, provided the enemy have presumption to favor us with an interview, which if they should think proper to do, the troops are in such high spirits that we will make an easy victory of them.

By this morning's order, the legion is to march at 5 o'clock.

Camp in sight of a British garrison, on the Miamis of the Lake, August 20th, 1794—*one hundred and fifty miles from Greenville.* This day the legion, after depositing every kind of baggage, took up the line of march at 7 o'clock, and continued their route down the margin of the river, without making any discovery, until 11 o'clock, when the front guard, which was composed of mounted volunteers, were fired on by the enemy. The guard retreated in the utmost confusion through the front guard of the regulars, commanded by Captain Cook and Lieutenant Steele, who, in spite of their utmost exertion, made a retreat. These fell in with the left of Captain Howell Lewis' company of light infantry and threw that part of the men into confusion, which Captain Lewis observing, he ordered the left of his company to retreat about forty yards, where he formed them and joined the right, which had stood their ground. They continued in this position until they were joined by part of Captain Springer's battalion of riflemen, which was nearly fifteen minutes after the firing commenced, who drove the enemy that had attempted to flank us on the right. Nearly at the same time, the right column came up, and the charge was sounded—the enemy gave way and fired scattering shots as they run off.

About the time the right column came up, a heavy firing took place on the left, which lasted but a short time, the enemy giving way in all quarters, which left us in possession of their *dead* to the number of forty. Our loss was thirty killed and one hundred wounded. Among the former we have to lament the loss of Captain Miss Campbell of the dragoons, and Lieutenant Henry B. Fowles of the 4th sub-legion; and of the latter, Captains Prior of the first, Slough of the fourth, and Van Rensselaer of the dragoons, also Lieutenant Campbell Smith of the fourth sub-legion. The whole loss of the enemy cannot at present be ascertained, but it is more than probable it must have been considerable, for we pursued them with rapidity for nearly two miles. As to the number of the enemy engaged in this action, opinions are so various that I am at a loss to know what to say; the most general opinion is one thousand five hundred, one-third of which are supposed to be Canadians; I am led to believe this number is not over the mark. After the troops had taken some refreshment, the legion continued their route down the river, and encamped in sight of the British garrison. One Canadian fell into our hands, who we loaded with irons.

Camp Foot of the Rapids, 21st August, 1794.—We are now lying within half a mile of a British garrison. A flag came to the commander-in-chief, the purport of which was that he, the commanding officer of the British fort, was surprised to see an American army so far advanced in this country; and why they had the assurance to encamp under the mouths of His Majesty's cannons! The commander-in-chief answered, that the affair of yesterday might well inform him why this army was encamped in its present position, and had the flying savages taken shelter under the walls of the fort, his Majesty's cannons should not have protected them.

Camp Foot of the Rapids, 22d August, 1794.—We have destroyed all the property within one hundred yards of the garrison. The volunteers were sent down eight miles below the fort, and have destroyed and burnt all the possessions belonging to the Canadians and savages. The commander-in-chief led his light infantry within pistol shot of the garrison to find out the strength and situation of the place, and in hopes of bringing a shot from our inveterate but silent enemies. They were too cowardly to come up to our expectations, and all we got by insulting the colors of Britain was a flag, the amount of which was, that the commanding officer of the fort felt himself as a soldier much injured by seeing His Majesty's colors insulted, and if such conduct was continued he would be under the necessity of making a proper resentment; upon which the commander-in-chief demanded the post, it being the right of the United States, which was refused. A small party of dragoons were sent over the river to burn and destroy all the houses, corn, etc., that were under cover of the fort, which was effected.

Camp Deposit, 23d August, 1794.—Having burned and destroyed everything contiguous to the fort without any opposition, the legion took up the line of march, and in the evening encamped on this ground, being the same they marched from the 20th. It may be proper to remark that we have heard nothing from the savages, or their allies the Canadians, since the action. The honors of war have been paid to the remains of those brave fellows who fell on the 20th, by a discharge of three rounds from sixteen pieces of ordnance, charged with shells. The ceremony was performed with the greatest solemnity.

Camp Thirty-two Mile Tree, 24*th August,* 1794.—The wounded being well provided for with carriages, etc., the legion took up the line of march, and halted in their old camp about 2 o'clock in the evening, without any accident. In this day's march we destroyed all the corn and burnt all the houses we met with, which were very considerable.

Camp Fifteen Mile Tree, 25*th August,* 1794.—The legion continued their march, and encamped on this ground at 3 o'clock P. M. This morning a few of the volunteers remained in the rear of the army, and soon after the legion took up their line of march they saw eight Indians coming into our camp; they fell in with them, killed one and wounded two.

Camp Nine Mile Tree, 26*th August,* 1794.—The legion continued their march, and after burning and destroying all the houses and corn on their route, arrived on this ground at 2 o'clock, being one of our encamping places when on our advance. All the wounded that were carried on litters and horseback were sent forward to Fort Defiance. Dr. Carmichael, through neglect, had the wounded men of the artillery and cavalry thrown into wagons, among spades, axes, picks, etc., in consequence of which the wounded are now lying in extreme pain, besides the frequent shocks of a wagon on the worst of roads. The wounded of the third sub-legion are under obligations to Dr. Haywood for his attention and humanity to them in their distress.

Camp Fort Defiance, 27*th August*, 1794.—The legion continued their route, and at 3 o'clock were encamped on the Miami, one mile above the garrison. On this day's march we destroyed all the corn and burnt all the houses on our route; the wounded are happily fixed in the garrison, and the doctors say there is no great danger of any of them dying.

Fort Defiance, 28*th August*, 1794.—The commander-in-chief thinks proper to continue on this ground for some time, to refresh the troops and send for supplies. There is corn, beans, pumpkins, etc., within four miles of this place, to furnish the troops three weeks.

"GENERAL ORDERS.—The Quartermaster General will issue "one gill of whisky to every man belonging to the Federal "army (this morning), as a small compensation for the fa- "tigues they have undergone for several days past. Major "General Scott will direct his quartermasters to attend accord- "ingly with their respective returns. The commander-in- "chief wishes it to be fairly understood that when he men- "tioned or may mention the Federal army in general orders, "that term comprehends and includes the legion and mounted "volunteers as one compound army; and that the term legion "comprehends the regular troops, agreeable to the organiza- "tion by the President of the United States, and by which "appellation they are known and recognized on all occasions "when acting by themselves, and separate from the mounted "volunteers. As the army will probably remain on this "ground for some time, vaults must be dug, and every pre- "caution taken to keep the encampment clean and healthy.

"The legion will be reviewed the day after to-morrow at 10 "o'clock. In the interim the arms must be clean and var- "nished, and the clothing of the soldier repaired and washed, "to appear in the most military condition possible; but in

"these necessary preparations for a review great caution must
"be used by the commanding officers of wings, not to permit
"too many men at one time to take their locks off, or to be
"engaged in washing.

"All the horses belonging to the quartermaster and con-
"tractor's department, in possession of the legion, must be
"returned this afternoon."

This is the first fair day we have had since we began to
return to this place, it having rained nearly constant for five
days, which was the occasion of fatiguing the troops very
much.

Fort Defiance, 29th August, 1794.—We are as yet encamped
on this ground; all the pack-horses belonging to the quartermaster and contractor's department moved this morning for
Fort Recovery, escorted by Brigadier General Todd's brigade
of mounted volunteers, for the purpose of bringing supplies to
this place. It is said the legion will continue in their present
camp until the return of this escort. Our spies were yesterday
twelve miles up this river, and they bring information that
the cornfields continue as far as they were up the river.

Fort Defiance, 30th August, 1794.—This day at 10 o'clock,
the commander- in-chief began to review the troops at the
posts occupied by the different corps, and I am led to believe
that he was well pleased at their appearance. Major Hughes,
Captain Slough, Captain Van Rensselaer and Lieutenant
Younghusband obtained a furlough to go home to repair their
healths, being, as they pretended, very much injured by the
service. I believe the two first and the last mentioned if they
never return will not be lamented by the majority of the army.

The out-guards were much alarmed this morning at the
mounted volunteers firing off all their arms without our having
any notice.

A

Headquarters, 31st August, 1794.—"GENERAL ORDERS.—
"general court-martial to consist of five members, will sit to-
"morrow morning at 10 o'clock, for the trial of such prisoners
"as may be brought before them. Major Shaylor, President,
"Lieutenant Wade, Judge Advocate.

"The disorderly and dangerous practice of permitting the
"soldiery to pass the chain of sentinels, on pretext of going
"after vegetables, can no longer be suffered. In future, on
"issuing day, only one man from each mess, properly armed,
"and commanded by the respective sub-legionary quarter-
"masters, will be sent as a detachment for vegetables, to
"march at 7 o'clock in the morning.

"The pack-horses shall forage daily under protection of a
"squadron of dragoons; every precaution must be taken to
"guard against surprise. Any non-commissioned officer or
"soldier found half a mile without the chain of sentinels,
"without a pass signed by the commanding officer of wings
"or sub-legion, or from headquarters, shall be deemed a
"deserter, and punished accordingly. Every sentinel suffering
"a non-commissioned officer or private to pass without such
"written permit, except a party on command, shall receive
"fifty lashes for each and every violation of this order.

"A fatigue party of three hundred non-commissioned officers
"and privates, with a proportion of commissioned officers,
"will parade at 7 o'clock to-morrow morning, furnished with
"one hundred axes, one hundred picks, and one hundred
"spades and shovels, with arms, commanded by Major
"Burbeck."

A part of this order was in consequence of three men of the
first sub-legion being either killed or taken by the enemy,
when out a foraging, which was done some time since, in a
very disorderly manner, at the same time liable to the attacks

15

of the enemy, without having it in their power to make the smallest resistance.

Fort Defiance, 1st September, 1794.—This morning the fatigue party ordered yesterday began to fortify and strengthen the fort and make it of sufficient strength to be proof against heavy metal : the work now on hand is a glascis with fascines, and a ditch twelve feet wide and eight feet deep ; the block-houses are to be made bomb-proof.

Fort Defiance, 2d September, 1794.—Every effective man of the light troops in the redoubts round the camp were ordered this morning to make three fascines.

The foraging party that went out this day brought in as much corn, dry enough to grate, as will suffice the troops three days. The soldiery get sick very fast with the fever and ague, and have it severely.

Fort Defiance, 3d September, 1794.—Nothing but hard fatigues going forward in all quarters. The garrison begins to put on the appearance of strength, and will in a few days be able to stand the shock of heavy cannon ; the troops are very sickly, and I believe the longer we continue in this place the worse it will be.

Fort Defiance, 4th September, 1794.—The number of our sick increases daily ; provision is nearly exhausted ; the whisky has been out for some time, which makes the hours pass heavily to the tune of Roslin Castle, when in our present situation they ought to go to the quick step of the merry man down to his grave. Hard duty and scanty allowance will cause an army to be low spirited, particularly the want of a little of the *wet.*

If it was not for the forage we get from the enemy's fields, the rations would not be sufficient to keep soul and body together.

Fort Defiance, 5th September, 1794.—No news of the escort; this day the troops drew no flour, and I fear we will shortly draw no beef; however, as long as the issuing of beef continues the troops will not suffer, as there is still corn in abundance on the river.

Fort Defiance, 6th September, 1794.—The work on the garrison goes on with life and will be completed in a few days. The weather very wet and cold; this morning there is a small frost.

Fort Defiance, 7th September, 1794.—Nothing of consequence took place this day. Our sick are getting better.

Fort Defiance, 8th September, 1794.—This day brings us information of the escort; by express we learn it will be with us to-morrow. It will be fortunate for us should provisions arrive, as we have not drawn any flour since the 7th instant; nevertheless we have the greatest abundance of vegetables.

Fort Defiance, 9th September, 1794.—The escort has not yet arrived, but will be in to-morrow. General Scott with the residue is ordered to march to-morrow morning at reveille. The commander-in-chief engaged with the volunteers to bring on the flour from Greenville on their own horses, for which they are to receive three dollars per hundred, delivered at the Miami villages.

Fort Defiance, 10th September, 1794.—The escort arrived this day about 3 o'clock, and brought with them two hundred kegs of flour and nearly two hundred head of cattle. Captain Preston and Ensigns Strother, Bowyer and Lewis, joined us this day with the escort. We received no liquor by this command, and I fancy we shall not receive any until we get into winter quarters, which will make the fatigues of the campaign appear double, as I am persuaded the troops would much rather live on half rations of beef and bread, provided they could obtain their full rations of whisky. The vegetables are as yet in the greatest abundance. The soldiers of Captain William Lewis's company are in perfect health, the wounded excepted.

Fort Defiance, 11th September, 1794.—This day General Barber's brigade of mounted volunteers marched for Fort Recovery for provisions, to meet us at the Miami villages by the 20th.

Fort Defiance, 12th September, 1794.—This day the pioneers were ordered to cut the road up the Miami under the direction of the sub-legionary quartermaster; they are to commence at 7 o'clock to-morrow morning.

Fort Defiance, 13th September, 1794.—This day a general order was issued, setting forth that the legion would march to-morrow morning precisely at 7 o'clock, every department to prepare themselves accordingly.

The squaw that Wells captured on the 11th August, was this day liberated and sent home. Three soldiers of the 1st and three of the 3d sub-legions deserted last night; sixteen volunteers pursued them; they are to receive twenty dollars if they bring them in dead or alive.

Camp 11½ *Mile Tree, 14th September,* 1794.—The legion began their march for the Miami villages at 7 o'clock this morning and encamped on this ground at 3 o'clock, after marching in the rain eight hours.

Camp 23d *Mile Tree, 15th September,* 1794.—The legion marched at 6 and encamped at 4 o'clock. Captain Preston, who commanded the light troops in the rear, got lost and lay out from the army all night with a large part of the baggage.

Camp 33d *Mile Tree, 16th September,* 1794.—We encamped on this ground at 4 o'clock, after passing over very rough roads, and woods thick with brush, the timber very lofty and the land generally rich and well watered.

Camp Miami Villages, 17th *September,* 1794.—The army halted on this ground at 5 o'clock, P. M., being 47 miles from Fort Defiance and 14 from our last encampment; there are nearly five hundred acres of cleared land lying in one body on the rivers St. Joseph, St. Mary's and the Miami; there are fine points of land contiguous to those rivers adjoining the cleared land. The rivers are navigable for small craft in the summer, and in the winter there is water sufficient for large boats, the land adjacent fertile and well timbered, and from every appearance it has been one of the largest settlements made by the Indians in this country.

Camp Miami Villages, 18th *September,* 1794.—This day the commander-in-chief reconnoitered the ground and determined on the spot to build a garrison on. The troops fortified their camps, as they halted too late yesterday to cover themselves. Four deserters from the British came to us this day; they bring information that the Indians are encamped eight miles below the British fort to the number of 1,600.

Camp Miami Villages, 19th *September,* 1794.—This day we hear that General Barber's brigade of mounted volunteers are within twelve miles of this place, and will be in early to-morrow with large supplies of flour; we have had heavy rains, the wind northwest, and the clouds have the appearance of emptying large quantities on this western world.

Camp Miami Villages, 20th *September,* 1794.—Last night it rained violently, and the wind blew from the northwest harder than I knew heretofore. General Barber with his command arrived in camp about 9 o'clock this morning with 553 kegs of flour, each containing 100 pounds.

Camp Miami Villages, 21st *September,* 1794.—The commander-in-chief reviewed the legion this day at 1 o'clock. All the quartermaster's horses set off this morning, escorted by the mounted volunteers, for Greenville, and are to return the soonest possible. We have not one quart of salt on this ground, which occasions bad and disagreeable living until the arrival of the next escort.

Camp Miami Villages, 22d September, 1794.—Nothing of consequence took place to-day, except that the troops drew no salt with their fresh provisions.

Camp Miami Villages, 23d September, 1794.—Four deserters from the British garrison arrived at our camp; they mention that the Indians are still embodied on the Miami, nine miles below the British fort; that they are somewhat divided in opinion—some are for peace and others for war.

Camp Miami Villages, 24th September, 1794.—This day the work commenced on the garrison, which I am apprehensive will take some time to complete it. A keg of whisky containing ten gallons was purchased this day for eighty dollars, a sheep for ten dollars; three dollars was offered for one pint of salt, but it could not be obtained for less than six.

Camp Miami Villages, 25th September, 1794.—Lieutenant Blue of the dragoons was this day arrested by ensign Johnson of the 4th S. L., but a number of their friends interfering the dispute was settled upon Lieutenant Blue's asking ensign Johnson's pardon.

Camp Miami Villages, 26th September, 1794.—McClelland, one of our spies, with a small party came in this evening from Fort Defiance, who brings information that the enemy are troublesome about the garrison, and that they have killed some of our men under the walls of the fort. Sixteen Indians were seen to-day near this place; a small party went in pursuit of them. I have not heard what discoveries they have made.

Camp Miami Villages, 27th September, 1794—No intelligence

of the enemy. The rain fell considerably last night; this morning the wind is southwest.

Camp Miami Villages, 28th September, 1794.—The weather proves colder.

Camp Miami Villages, 30th September, 1794.—Salt and whisky were drawn by the troops this day, and a number of the soldiery became much intoxicated, they having stolen a quantity of liquor from the quartermaster.

Camp Miami Villages, 1st October, 1794.— The volunteers appear to be uneasy, and have refused to do duty. They are ordered by the commander-in-chief to march to-morrow for Greenville to assist the pack-horses, which I am told they are determined not to do.

Camp Miami Villages, 2d October, 1794.—This morning the volunteers refused to go on command, and demanded of General Scott to conduct them home; he ordered them to start with General Barber, or if they made the smallest delay they should lose all their pay and be reported to the war office as revolters. This had the desired effect, and they went off, not in good humor.

Camp Miami Villages, 3d October, 1794.—Every officer, non-commissioned officer and soldier belonging to the square are on fatigue this day, hauling trees on the hind wheels of wagons; the first day we got an extra gill per man, which appears to be all the compensation at this time in the power of the commander-in-chief to make the troops.

Camp Miami Villages, 4th October, 1794.—This morning we had the hardest frost I ever saw in the middle of December; it was like a small snow; there was ice in our camp-kettles three-fourths of an inch thick. The fatigues. go on with velocity, considering the rations the troops are obliged to live on.

Camp Miami Villages, 5th October, 1794.— The weather ex

tremely cold, and hard frosts—the wind northwest. Everything quiet, and nothing but harmony and peace throughout
the camp, which is something uncommon.

Camp Miami Villages, 6th October, 1794.—Plenty and quiet-
ness, the same as yesterday. The volunteers engaged to work
on the garrison, for which they are to receive three gills of
whisky per man per day; their employment is digging the
ditch and filling up the parapet.

Camp Miami Villages, 7th October, 1794.— The volunteers
are soon tired of work, and have refused to labor any longer;
they have stolen and killed seventeen beeves in the course of
these two days past.

Camp Miami Villages, 8th October, 1794.—The troops drew
but half rations of flour this day. The cavalry and other
horses die very fast—not less than four or five per day.

Camp Miami Villages, 9th October, 1794.— The volunteers
have agreed to build a block-house in front of the garrison.

Camp Miami Villages, 11th October, 1794.—A Canadian [Ro-
zelle] with a flag arrived this evening; his business was to
deliver up three prisoners in exchange for his brother, who
was taken on the 20th August. He brings information that
the Indians are in council with Girty and McKee near the
fort of Detroit; that all the tribes are for peace except the
Shawanese, who are determined to prosecute the war.

Camp Miami Villages, 12th October, 1794.—The mounted volunteers of Kentucky marched for Greenville, to be mustered
and dismissed the service of the United States army, they
being of no further service therein.

Camp Miami Villages, 13th October, 1794.—Captain Gibson
marched this day, and took with him a number of horses for
Fort Recovery to receive supplies of provisions.

Camp Miami Villages, 14th October, 1794.—Nothing particular this day.

Camp Miami Villages, 15th October, 1794.— The Canadian that came in on the 11th left us this day, accompanied by his brother; they have promised to furnish the garrison at Defiance with stores at a moderate price, which, if performed, will be a great advantage to the officers and soldiers of that post.

Camp Miami Villages, 16th October, 1794.— Nothing new; weather wet and cold—wind from the northwest. The troops healthy in general.

Camp Miami Villages, 17th October, 1794.—This day Captain Gibson arrived with a large quantity of flour, beef and sheep.

Camp Miami Villages, 18th October, 1794.—Captain Springer and Brock, with 'all the pack-horses, marched with the cavalry this morning for Greenville, and the foot for Recovery, the latter to return with the smallest delay with a supply of provisions for this post and Defiance.

Camp Miami Villages, 19th October, 1794.— This day the troops were not ordered for labor, being the first day for four weeks, and accordingly attended divine service.

Camp Miami Villages, 20th October, 1794.— An express arrived this day with dispatches to the commander-in-chief; the contents are kept secret.

A court-martial to sit this day for the trial of Lieutenant Charles Hyde.

Camp Miami Villages, 21st October, 1794.—This day were read the proceedings of a general court-martial held on Lieutenant Charles Hyde (yesterday), was found not guilty of the charges exhibited against him, and was therefore acquitted.

Camp Miami Villages, 22d October, 1794.—This morning at 7 o'clock the following companies, under the command of Lieutenant Colonel Commandant Hamtramck of the 1st sublegion, took possession of this place, viz: Captain Kingsbury's 1st; Captain Greaton's 2d; Captain Spark's and Captain

Reed's, 3d; Captain Preston's 4th; and Captain Porter's of artillery; and after firing fifteen rounds of cannon, Colonel Hamtramck gave it the name of Fort Wayne.

Camp Miami Villages, 23d October, 1794.—The general fatigue of the garrison ended this day, and Colonel Hamtramck, with the troops under his command, to furnish it as he may think fit. All the soldiers' huts are completed except covering, and the weather is favorable for that work.

Camp Miami Villages, 24th October, 1794.—This day the troops drew but half rations of beef and flour, the beef very bad.

Camp Miami Villages, 25th October, 1794.—Nothing extraordinary the same as yesterday.

This evening Captain Springer with the escort arrived, with a supply of flour and salt. A Frenchman and a half Indian came to headquarters, but where they are from or their business we cannot learn but that it is of a secret nature.

Camp Miami Villages, 26th October, 1794.—Nothing occurring to-day except an expectation to march the day after to-morrow.

Camp Miami Villages, 27th October, 1794.—Agreeable to general orders of this day, we will march for Greenville to-morrow morning at 8 o'clock.

Camp nine miles from Fort Wayne, 28th October, 1794.—The legion took up the line of march at 9 o'clock and arrived here without anything particular occurring.

Camp twenty-one miles from Fort Wayne, 29th October, 1794. The troops proceeded on their march at sunrise, and arrived on this ground at half past 3 o'clock, our way was through rich and well timbered land, the weather cold and much like for rain.

Camp Southwest side of St. Mary's river, 30th October, 1794. The legion proceeded on ther march at 7 o'clock, and arrived here at sunset; continual heavy rain all day.

Camp Girty's Town, 31*st October*, 1794.—The troops took up their line of march at sunrise, and arrived here three hours after night, through heavy rain.

Greenville, 2*nd November*, 1794.—This evening the legion arrived here, where they marched from 28th July, 1794.

We were saluted with twenty-four rounds from a six-pounder. Our absence from this ground amounted to three months and six days. And so ends the expedition of General Wayne's campaign.

The First American Frontier
AN ARNO PRESS/NEW YORK TIMES COLLECTION

Agnew, Daniel.
A History of the Region of Pennsylvania North of the
Allegheny River. 1887.

Alden, George H.
New Government West of the Alleghenies Before 1780. 1897.

Barrett, Jay Amos.
Evolution of the Ordinance of 1787. 1891.

Billon, Frederick.
Annals of St. Louis in its Early Days Under the French
and Spanish Dominations. 1886.

Billon, Frederick.
Annals of St. Louis in its Territorial Days, 1804-1821. 1888.

Littel, William.
Political Transactions in and Concerning Kentucky. 1926.

Bowles, William Augustus.
Authentic Memoirs of William Augustus Bowles. 1916.

Bradley, A. G.
The Fight with France for North America. 1900.

Brannan, John, ed.
Official Letters of the Military and Naval Officers of the
War, 1812-1815. 1823.

Brown, John P.
Old Frontiers. 1938.

Brown, Samuel R.
The Western Gazetteer. 1817.

Cist, Charles.
Cincinnati Miscellany of Antiquities of the West and Pioneer History. (2 volumes in one). 1845-6.

Claiborne, Nathaniel Herbert.
Notes on the War in the South with Biographical Sketches of the Lives of Montgomery, Jackson, Sevier, and Others. 1819.

Clark, Daniel.
Proofs of the Corruption of Gen. James Wilkinson. 1809.

Clark, George Rogers.
Colonel George Rogers Clark's Sketch of His Campaign in the Illinois in 1778-9. 1869.

Collins, Lewis.
Historical Sketches of Kentucky. 1847.

Cruikshank, Ernest, ed,
Documents Relating to Invasion of Canada and the Surrender of Detroit. 1912.

Cruikshank, Ernest, ed,
The Documentary History of the Campaign on the Niagara Frontier, 1812-1814. (4 volumes). 1896-1909.

Cutler, Jervis.
A Topographical Description of the State of Ohio, Indian Territory, and Louisiana. 1812.

Cutler, Julia P.
The Life and Times of Ephraim Cutler. 1890.

Darlington, Mary C.
History of Col. Henry Bouquet and the Western Frontiers of Pennsylvania. 1920.

Darlington, Mary C.
Fort Pitt and Letters From the Frontier. 1892.

De Schweinitz, Edmund.
The Life and Times of David Zeisberger. 1870.

Dillon, John B.
History of Indiana. 1859.

Eaton, John Henry.
Life of Andrew Jackson. 1824.

English, William Hayden.
Conquest of the Country Northwest of the Ohio. (2 volumes in one). 1896.

Flint, Timothy.
Indian Wars of the West. 1833.

Forbes, John.
Writings of General John Forbes Relating to His Service in North America. 1938.

Forman, Samuel S.
Narrative of a Journey Down the Ohio and Mississippi in 1789-90. 1888.

Haywood, John.
Civil and Political History of the State of Tennessee to 1796. 1823.

Heckewelder, John.
History, Manners and Customs of the Indian Nations. 1876.

Heckewelder, John.
Narrative of the Mission of the United Brethren. 1820.

Hildreth, Samuel P.
Pioneer History. 1848.

Houck, Louis.
The Boundaries of the Louisiana Purchase: A Historical Study. 1901.

Houck, Louis.
History of Missouri. (3 volumes in one). 1908.

Houck, Louis.
The Spanish Regime in Missouri. (2 volumes in one). 1909.

Jacob, John J.
A Biographical Sketch of the Life of the Late Capt. Michael Cresap. 1826.

Jones, David.
A Journal of Two Visits Made to Some Nations of Indians on the West Side of the River Ohio, in the Years 1772 and 1773. 1774.

Kenton, Edna.
Simon Kenton. 1930.

Loudon, Archibald.
Selection of Some of the Most Interesting Narratives of Outrages. (2 volumes in one). 1808-1811.

Monette, J. W.
History, Discovery and Settlement of the Mississippi Valley. (2 volumes in one). 1846.

Morse, Jedediah.
American Gazetteer. 1797.

Pickett, Albert James.
History of Alabama. (2 volumes in one). 1851.

Pope, John.
A Tour Through the Southern and Western Territories. 1792.

Putnam, Albigence Waldo.
History of Middle Tennessee. 1859.

Ramsey, James G. M.
Annals of Tennessee. 1853.

Ranck, George W.
Boonesborough. 1901.

Robertson, James Rood, ed.
Petitions of the Early Inhabitants of Kentucky to the Gen. Assembly of Virginia. 1914.

Royce, Charles.
Indian Land Cessions. 1899.

Rupp, I. Daniel.
History of Northampton, Lehigh, Monroe, Carbon and Schuykill Counties. 1845.

Safford, William H.
The Blennerhasset Papers. 1864.

St. Clair, Arthur.
A Narrative of the Manner in which the Campaign Against the Indians, in the Year 1791 was Conducted. 1812.

Sargent, Winthrop, ed.
A History of an Expedition Against Fort DuQuesne in 1755. 1855.

Severance, Frank H.
An Old Frontier of France. (2 volumes in one). 1917.

Sipe, C. Hale.
Fort Ligonier and Its Times. 1932.

Stevens, Henry N.
Lewis Evans: His Map of the Middle British Colonies in America. 1920.

Timberlake, Henry.
The Memoirs of Lieut. Henry Timberlake. 1927.

Tome, Philip.
Pioneer Life: Or Thirty Years a Hunter. 1854.

Trent, William.
Journal of Captain William Trent From Logstown to Pickawillany. 1871.

Walton, Joseph S.
Conrad Weiser and the Indian Policy of Colonial Pennsylvania. 1900.

Withers, Alexander Scott.
Chronicles of Border Warfare. 1895.